How to Give Your Best Speech or Presentation Ever

A Step-by-Step Manual for Speaking in Public

ISBN: 1-4392-3333-0
ISBN-13: 9781439233337

To order additional copies, please contact us.
BookSurge
www.booksurge.com
1-866-308-6235
orders@booksurge.com

How to Give Your Best Speech or Presentation Ever

A Step-by-Step Manual for Speaking in Public

Greg Ferguson

BookSurge

2009

Dedication

To my wife Stacey, and our children Zach, Natalie, and Wyatt:

Thank you for believing in me.

Table of Contents

Introduction

This book is for the occasional speaker. Whether you speak once a decade or several times a year, this book will give you everything you need to know to give a great presentation. This book will show you how to plan, prepare, practice, and polish a speech or presentation lasting anywhere from one minute to a whole day. It will help you become a better speaker so that you can communicate better to groups ranging from a few people to several hundred.

The ability to speak in front of a group is as important today as it was in Aristotle's time. Today, we have new tools and multiple types of media such as PowerPoint and imbedded video to help enhance our messages. Yet every day there are speeches that have the same common problems: they are too long, they are boring, they have no flow, they try to cover too much information, or they are not audience focused. Sometimes speeches do not even have a discernable purpose. Even with modern enhancements, messages still may not get through.

The ability to deliver a message well in person is still a crucial skill in our business and personal lives. Being able to speak effectively will enhance your ability to communicate, help advance your career or purpose, and assist your organization achieve its goals.

There are many books on how to speak in public. Why do I feel the need to write another? Because I have come to learn that there is a repeatable process to giving a great presentation, and I have not seen another book break it down into its component parts as this book does. This book is divided into two parts:

- Part One of this book will break down this repeatable process into ten Critical Steps. These steps are just as critical for the beginning speaker as they are for a professional speaker.
- Part Two provides strategies and tactics to help you give your best possible performance. These strategies and tactics teach you how to deliver your message with maximum impact.

If you read and apply the Critical Steps in Part One of this book, you should be able to give a basic speech and get your point across. The content will be solid and will convey your message in a format that the audience will comprehend. If you read and apply Part Two of this book after following Part One, you will be able to give a great presentation no matter what your skill level is and no matter how nervous you think you might get.

The information in this book is a collection of knowledge that I have assembled over more than 20 years of speaking in public and teaching in different capacities. I have taught classes on presentation skills and have witnessed thousands of presentations ranging from outstanding to awful. I have seen some first time speakers give fantastic performances, and I have seen some veteran speakers make the most basic critical errors. I have studied the structures and tactics of classic speeches throughout the centuries, distilled the methods to find their commonalities, and applied my own experience to produce a course of instruction that will help anyone wanting to improve their public speaking skills.

People who have followed the steps and strategies in this book have told me that they are far more prepared and far less nervous about speaking than they ever knew they could be. I know that you can, too. So get ready to learn how to give your best presentation ever!

Author's note: The word speech might imply an event where someone speaks without the use of any aids while a presentation uses aids of some kind. The terms "speech" and "presentation" are used interchangeably in this book.

Part One:

Planning and Preparing

Critical Step 1: Have a plan before you begin

In order to make the most efficient use of your planning and preparation time, and in order to produce the best possible speech or presentation, you need a game plan or a process to follow. This book provides that plan. It will show you the steps to prepare your speech and how to accomplish each step.

Tactic: Have a process and stick to it

Along with having a process to follow, it is important to know why the steps are in the order they are placed. For example, beginning with the end in mind is very important at the outset of your planning because without it, you may not have a clear understanding of what you are researching. I have heard hundreds of speeches where I could not determine the purpose of the speech. If you don't know the purpose of your speech, there is no way your audience will, either.

Another example of the importance of the order of planning is to develop the body of your speech before you try to write the introduction. If you try to write the introduction first, several things can happen:

- You can end up putting too much information in the introduction
- You will almost certainly have to rewrite the introduction after your speech takes shape
- You may lock yourself into a format that does not convey the material in an optimal way
- You may be stifled in your thought process, brainstorming, or research

An added benefit of writing the introduction after writing the body of the speech is that it will be much easier to write once the body is finished.

Part One of this book will go through the steps in the Planning and Preparation stages required to create an outstanding presentation in the order they need to be done. The Practicing stage, which includes sharpening your delivery skills, can be done in any order. These are found in Part Two of this book.

Tactic: Allocate time to plan, prepare, and practice

It makes sense to have a *timeline* beginning on the day you start planning and ending on the day you give your presentation. This is important because you do not want the preparation phase to run into the morning of the speech, leaving you little or no time to practice. There are three distinct phases of the creation of a speech: planning, preparing, and practicing. A guideline to the amount of time you should spend on each phase is as follows:

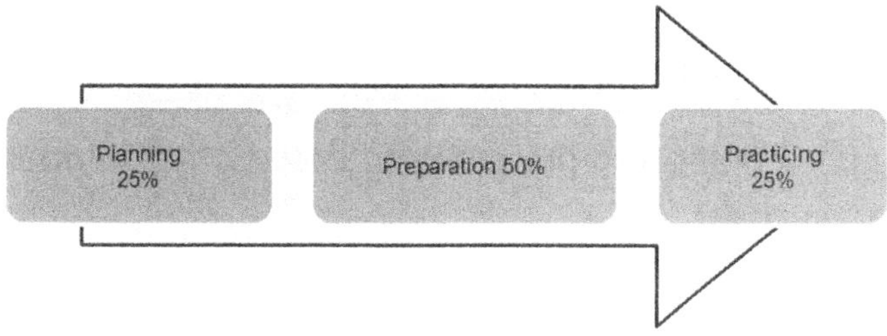

Timeline

The planning phase consists of four Critical Steps 1-4:

- Step 1: Have a plan before you begin
- Step 2: Establish your purpose
- Step 3: Determine "What's in it for them?"
- Step 4: Brainstorm

The preparation phase consists of Critical Steps 5-10:

- Step 5: Determine your presentation structure
- Step 6: Use smooth transitions
- Step 7: Create a dynamite opening
- Step 8: Be smart with visual aids
- Step 9: Add dimension
- Step 10: Conclude with strength

The practicing phase consists of three parts:

- Practice
- Practice

- Practice

The amount of time spent in each phase can vary from presentation to presentation based on a number of factors such as:

- Amount of information already available
- Purpose of the presentation
- Knowledge level of speaker
- Knowledge level of audience
- Length of presentation

No matter what the scenario, do not underestimate the time needed to practice. Try to determine how much time you plan to each of the areas. The amount of time you eventually spend in each area may change slightly from your original estimate, but thinking it through ahead of time will keep you from spending too much time in the planning and preparation phases at the expense of the practice phase. Not spending enough time in the planning stage can lead to a presentation without a defined purpose, or it can lead to a presentation with too much or too little information. If you spend too little time in the preparation phase, your presentation may be disjointed and hard to follow. Too little time practicing can result in a great speech with a mediocre delivery. We will cover practicing in detail in Part Two of this book.

Critical Step 2: Establish your purpose

What is it that you want your audience to get from your speech? What is your purpose? Why have you been asked to speak? There are many reasons you might be speaking to your audience. The four most popular reasons are:

- To inform
- To entertain
- To motivate
- To persuade

Is your speech to give an update? To give a call to action? To tell a story? To sell an idea? Certainly these reasons can overlap. It is quite possible to entertain an audience while trying to persuade them.

If there is "one main thing" you want your audience to remember, to do, or take action on—what is it? This is the heart of your presentation. Do you want your homeowners' association to install a playground? Do you want people to invest in your company? Do you want the city council to prevent a dump from being built in your back yard? As you do your research and put your presentation together, stay focused on the heart of your presentation.

It is very possible that your purpose or the heart of your presentation could change during your planning or preparation stages. If this happens, ensure that your supporting materials reflect the change so that the message in the body of your speech is not confusing or diluted. For example, the heart of your presentation may be to get investors *to give you money* when you begin planning your presentation. Upon refinement, after following the steps in this book, you may find the heart is to convince the audience that *it is in their best interest* to invest in your company. There is a big difference between these two concepts, and your presentation will change as a result.

Tactic: Stay focused

Keeping the heart of your presentation in mind as you go through the planning, preparation, and practicing stages of creating your presentation will do the following:

- Keep the audience engaged
- Keep you focused on your message
- Prevent you from wandering during your speech
- Provide logical structure to your presentation
- Make your presentation more memorable
- Help you achieve the purpose of your presentation

Tactic: Make them remember

If the audience can remember the heart of your presentation a week after your speech, you have succeeded.

However, sometimes, the main thing an audience remembers may be different than you intended. A few years ago, I went to an international convention and heard some of the most sought after speakers in the country. I went to one presentation that I remember as being very entertaining and enjoyable. The thing I can still remember the most from this speech was how to peel a banana. Now, the subject of the speech, as I recall, had something to do with the top 10 things about something. I don't remember what they were, but I remember the banana. I went to another presentation where the motivational speaker emphasized not letting others bring your attitude down. I can still hear his message in my mind as I write this. If the first speaker had sharpened the message to reinforce the heart of the presentation, or taught me to remember what the heart was during the speech, I might remember it better today.

Critical Step 3: Determine "What's in it for them?"

Once you have determined the purpose of your speech, it is imperative that you determine: "What is in it for your audience?" To answer this question, ask yourself the following:

- Why should they care about what you are presenting?
- What are their motivations?
- What are their key wants, needs, or desires?
- How can you help them?

For example, suppose you start out with the intention of getting more money for your department, group, organization, etc. You can give a fantastic presentation, but unless you connect it to the needs, wants, or desires of your audience, your presentation will not get the results you want. Often a presenter will go on and on about themselves, their product, or their company while the audience is thinking "So what?" or "This is no different from the last person that was in here."

Tactic: Determine the benefits for your audience

You may talk about how great you are or how wonderful your company is, but the audience won't care until they can see how it benefits them. A common symptom of this type of thinking is when a presenter begins to list or state a long list of features related to the subject. These are may be nice, but unless they transfer to value to the listener, they really don't matter.

Sometimes salespeople get caught in the same trap. They might start talking about the features of an item before thinking about how they will benefit the buyer. I remember many years ago when I was shopping for a car and the salesperson kept telling me all about car seats, occupant safety, luggage room—all things that a family might find important. I was unmarried in my early 20's. He was clearly naming the features, but not determining how they would benefit me.

Consider the following examples:

Features	Benefits
Faster	Higher Customer Satisfaction
Higher Quality	Lower Return Rate
Cheaper	Higher Market Penetration
Safer	Lower Insurance Costs
Greener	Qualify For Grants

In the examples shown, the benefits are only benefits if you already know ahead of time that they are benefits to the listeners. Otherwise, they may only be features. If a lower return rate or a higher market penetration is not important to your audience, it is only a feature.

In order to determine what a benefit is for your audience, you will need to ensure you know your audience as well as you can. There are hundreds of things to find out about your audience, but the following are good places to start:

- What are the demographics such as age, income, gender, education?
- What are their occupations—are they all engineers, advertising executives, etc.?
- What are their positions?
- What is their knowledge level of your subject?
- Why are they listening to you?
- What issues are they facing as a group or individually?
- How can you help them fix their problems or achieve their goals?
- What do the members of the group have in common—are they all parents, volunteers, investors, donors, employees of the same company, etc.?

Once you gather some of the information above, you can start thinking about how your presentation can benefit your audience. This analysis will also help later in your preparation by helping you determine the kind of information you present to your audience and how you present it.

You may be thinking at this point, "My purpose has more than one part," or "I want the audience to remember more than one thing." Perhaps you offer many benefits in your presentation. That is fine at this point, but you need to be thinking about how to package your list of benefits to get one main benefit for the purpose of your presentation. The body of your presentation (covered later) will support your purpose.

Critical Step 4: Brainstorm

The brainstorm step of creating your presentation can take anywhere from a few hours to a few weeks, depending on a number of factors such as:

- How long you have to prepare
- How much you already know about your subject
- How much your audience already knows about your subject
- How much you don't know about your subject
- How many people will be involved in the process

Once you know the date of your presentation, determine how much time you will spend in the brainstorming mode. If all of your information is already available, the brainstorming time is still very valuable in helping determine what parts or how much of the information you will use.

How much time should you allocate to brainstorming? If you need to give your presentation in a month, perhaps a week in the brainstorming mode will be appropriate. If you have a week, perhaps a day or day and a half will do it. There is no set rule of thumb, but the brainstorming step is crucial in gathering your material.

Tactic: Brainstorming as a group

If you will have a group working on your presentation or if you will have people helping you prepare, a formal brainstorming session will be very beneficial. Formal brainstorming is used for things as diverse as strategic planning or coming up with an advertising campaign. No matter what the goal, brainstorming helps come up with as many ideas as possible in a finite period of time.

A group brainstorming session will have several people in a room all coming up with ideas and writing them down on flip charts, a white board, or on Post-it™ notes. When you are ready to begin brainstorming, take your purpose or your "one main thing" and get as many ideas as possible on it. There are a few common rules associated with formal brainstorming:

- Generate only basic ideas and concepts
- Do not discuss ideas
- List ideas without judgment
- Emphasize quantity
- Encourage all comments and encourage all to participate
- Build on others' ideas
- Have no set format for the flow of ideas

You may decide to appoint a facilitator to encourage ideas or help expand on the ideas presented. This facilitator should ask questions to provoke further thought on the ideas presented. This facilitator should also keep the session on track by keeping the participants from getting to get too focused on one idea or trying to solve a problem. Brainstorming may not come naturally to some that like to solve problems, so it is imperative to stay on track. Once the initial wave of mental energy has diminished in any area, the facilitator should ask probing questions about other ideas or concepts.

When the ideas begin to slow down, it is like when popcorn is about done popping. There may be a kernel or two left to pop, but you need to stop cooking.

Once the ideas have stopped "popping" the participants begin to group the ideas around central concepts. If the notes are on Post-it™ notes, put them all on a table or on a wall and group have the participants start grouping them by affinity. This means put the ideas that seem to go together near one another. This will yield some obvious groups, but a few ideas may still be homeless. Don't worry about that at this point. Once you get your ideas into groups, you are beginning to form the main points of your presentation.

Tactic: Brainstorm solo

Perhaps you will be giving your presentation on your own and do not have a team to help you brainstorm. When you know you will be giving a presentation soon, ideas will come to you at all times. As in formal brainstorming, do not try to qualify the ideas at this stage. Ideas may or may not prove to be relevant later, but get everything down.

Make it a practice to carry around a notepad, yellow pad, or even a single piece of paper for jotting down things as they come to you. In the past, I have carried around a tattered piece of yellow pad paper in my pocket for up to three or four weeks so I could write down ideas as they came to me at any time of the day. You might even put the pad or paper next to your bed in the event an idea comes to you as you try to fall asleep, or even if one comes to you in a dream. It is like having a computer program running in the background all the time. Be ready when the ideas come to you.

You can also keep notes on your personal digital assistant. You can even send yourself a text message or email every time you think of something. Any of these methods will act as long as you capture the ideas as they come to you.

Once you approach the end of your solo brainstorming period, prepare to assemble your ideas into groups in the same manner as group brainstorming. You can put each idea onto a Post-it™ note and scatter them on a table or wall, or you can take a sheet of paper for each potential group and transfer the ideas onto one of the sheets until your list is completely grouped. Of course, you can keep all of your ideas on a computer, but many people find the sorting process easier if they can physically manipulate the data.

This is the method I used to write this book. I carried around yellow pad papers for weeks and jotted down ideas as they came to me, as I gave presentations, and as I observed others giving presentations. When I did not have the papers with me, I sent myself an email with my phone. Once I gathered the majority of the ideas, I grouped the ideas into categories that eventually became the chapters of this book.

Tactic: Involve others

Perhaps you work in a large company where others can help, but you are unable to assemble a formal brainstorming session. You can still benefit from the input of others by stating your purpose and letting others know that you will be giving the presentation at a certain date. Ask for input on what they think should be included in your presentation. If you work in a particular department, you can solicit ideas from different departments. If you work in a non-profit organization, you can get input from different committees. As you get feedback, you can create a separate folder on your computer for the feedback, or you can transfer the ideas individually to your working papers.

Tactic: Group your ideas

Whether you do group brainstorming, solo brainstorming, or a combination of the two, conclude by grouping the ideas into what appear to be their natural groupings or clusters. Once you have them arranged, ask yourself if this is the only way they can be grouped. For example, can the groupings be rearranged as geographic, departmental, chronological, or some other way?

The groupings may start to look something like this:

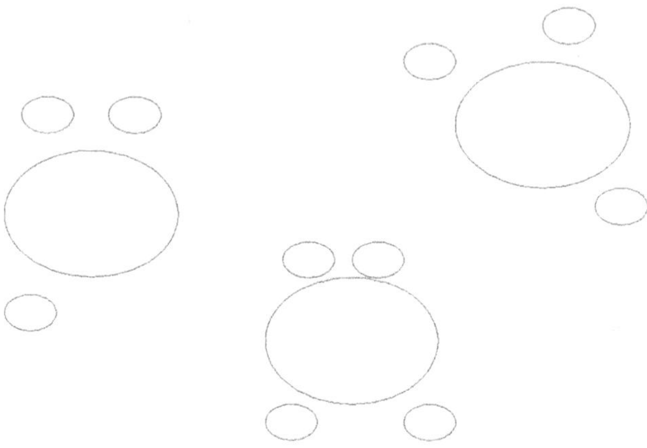

Or they may look something like this:

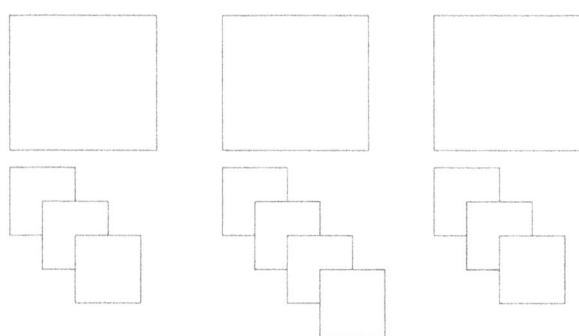

The way you group your ideas will form the structure of the body of your presentation. We will look at how to structure the body of your presentation in the next chapter.

Tactic: Follow up brainstorming with research

Once you have neared the end of your brainstorming time, you may find that you need to augment your concepts with additional research. The amount of research you need to do may be influenced by:

- Your existing knowledge of the topic
- The amount of time you have to prepare
- The expected length of your presentation
- The level of detail you will need to present
- The knowledge level of your audience

You may end up with much more information than you need. Some of the information you gather may not make it into your presentation. Keep in mind that it is easier to edit the information down in the planning and preparation phases than to attempt to pump it up later or try to wing it on presentation day.

Critical Step 5: Determine your structure

There are numerous ways or methods to structure the body of your presentation. The way you group or sort the information in the main body of your presentation will need to support or prove your purpose. The groups of information you get from brainstorming and research become the "bones" of your presentation. These bones will form the skeleton of your presentation that will provide a structure to support its heart or main purpose.

We will cover the most common ways to group or organize your information here. Many other methods are simply variations of the ones we will cover. In some cases, you may find a combination of methods will work best for your presentation.

Chronological. This method is very easy for telling a story or presenting the history of a group or organization. If the purpose of a presentation is to only inform the audience on how the presenter got to where he is today, this is a very logical way to present information. This method may also inspire an audience.

Suppose the founder of a company is trying to persuade a group to invest in his company. A chronological approach can give a good summary of the progression of the company from its inception. The information identified in the brainstorming step of preparation might be critical decision points in the history of the company or they may be significant milestones such as sales levels or number of employees. In any case, the timeline should be easy to follow and the result should prove the point that an investment in the company satisfies the need of the investment group.

Spatial. A spatial presentation is a presentation that groups ideas visually. Its power is comparing how the components relate to one another physically. While it is a good way to inform the audience of physical relationships, it will need more to motivate or persuade. Some ways to compare things spatially are:

- Big to small
- Top to bottom
- Left to right
- Upstairs and downstairs

Suppose an architect is presenting a concept of a new building. A spatial presentation might start out with exterior views, move into the interior, and then go from floor to floor or room to room. The spatial method can move an audience through a presentation very effectively. Of course, the end result should not be to show how great the structure is, but how well it fulfills the needs of the customer.

Spatial could be a bit more abstract, such as in the following diagram:

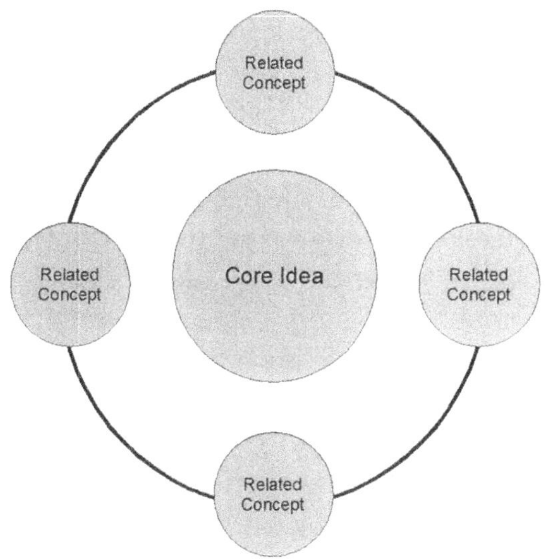

Spatial Diagram

Geographic. Geographic groupings are easy to comprehend and are excellent for informing an audience. Geographic can be organized by:

- City, state, or country
- Continent
- Region or territory
- East to West, North to South

This format is useful for sales or production updates. If a company or organization has multiple locations, it may be the easiest way to present information. This method can also be used in conjunction with other methods listed below, such as Problem/Solution, Numerical, Compare/Contrast, and others.

Features and Benefits. This can be very powerful for motivating or persuading. The presenter can take information and apply it directly to the needs, wants, and desires of the audience—if the presenter has done a good job of getting to know the audience. This is highly effective in most sales presentations and is applicable to presentations about products or services. The features and benefits method can also be used to promote a concept or proposal. Perhaps a homeowner would like to convince her homeowners' association to upgrade the signs and monumentation in her neighborhood. She could structure her presentation so that her main points center on the reasons the homeowners would benefit from investing in her proposal.

Compare/Contrast. In this method, the presentation is taking several attributes of the subject (often the company or product highlighted in the presentation) and comparing them to the attributes of another. Typically the one being compared is a competitor or alternate choice for the audience.

Many people in research and development positions use this format to make presentations. For example, a project manager for a drug manufacturer may propose a new product. Comparing and contrasting the new product to one or more existing products might be a very effective way to convince the members of the audience to move forward with continued funding of the new product.

Numerical. A numerical structure uses a list as a way to group information. This is often the top ten reasons for something or the five best ways to do something. This has become a popular method because:

- It is very easy to follow
- Can be used in many different environments
- It is easy to prepare

Sometimes the numerical method may be a method of last resort. It is useful for ideas that may not connect together well with other methods. If you found it difficult to group your ideas in the brainstorming stage, this may work well for you. Caution: don't exceed ten items in a presentation. David Letterman made his top ten list popular, but even ten is a lot to cover in a presentation. It is very difficult to take away ten main supporting points of the "one main thing" in a presentation.

Question/Answer. This method is used if the audience has a basic knowledge of the information being presented. This approach is not to be confused with a question and answer session at the end of a presentation. In that case, the questions are from the audience. In this method, the presenter asks the questions and then answers them. This structure can do a good job of informing, and done well, it can do a good job of persuading.

An example where this type of presentation could be effective is for a school system that is considering redistricting its students. The members of the audience may already know that they are being redistricted to a new school, but want to know things such as:

- Why does the school system need to redistrict now?
- Why is my neighborhood affected?
- Will there be bus service and at what times?
- Do I have any choices in the matter?
- What happens if I want my children to stay at their current school?

The presenter could make the presentation with the expected or most common questions and then present the answers. This is similar to FAQs (Frequently Asked Questions) on websites.

Departmental. This method is generally used for updating the audience. It can be very informative, but it does not often do a good job of entertaining, motivating, or persuading. This can be used in conjunction with the geographic method.

For example, if a company has locations in different cities, the presentation could cover each city then break each city down by department such as sales, production, finance, etc. This creates an orderly presentation, but is of little use beyond informing.

Problem or Challenge/Solution. This way of presenting can be very effective in motivating or persuading since it works well with identifying needs and addressing them. This method is popular in fields where innovation moves very quickly. For example, it works well with software products or medical devices.

If a medical device company sells stents for patients with strokes and aneurisms to hospitals, an effective presentation would show how a new product addresses the major known problems of the current stents. The groups that were identified in the brainstorming step would be the current major problems, and the presentation would then focus on solutions to each problem.

General to Specific. This method is useful for bringing an audience to a common point. If the audience has varying levels of knowledge of your subject, this can be very effective for getting everyone to a decision point if it is done well. This is also known as Big Picture to Little Picture.

If the director of a municipal library system proposes to open a new branch, she may use the general to specific method of organization. She may start out by talking about reading trends in the United States, move to bookstore sales, then to library usage throughout the country. She could then talk about the local system and its statistics. Finally, she would use the facts to point toward the need for a new branch. This method can be used actively or passively. This means you can tell your audience that you are moving from general to specific, or you can just start out with the general and move to the specific. Either way, the audience is moved through the information like a funnel to the heart of your presentation as in the diagram that follows:

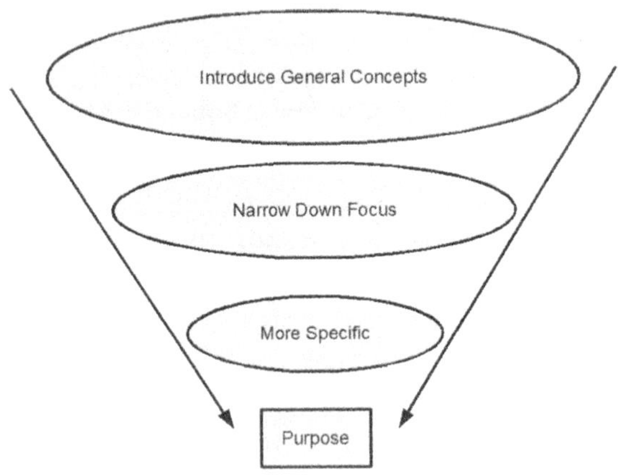

Example of General to Specific Structure

Objections/Answers. Similar to Question/Answer, this method anticipates or addresses objections and attempts to persuade the audience. It is also very useful for informing an audience. Using this method implies that you already know what the objections are or might be. This is also very useful for controversial subjects or subjects where there is known opposition.

Let's say the Department of Transportation plans on putting a new road or highway through a rural area. The engineers may have already done a significant amount of planning and found that the proposed path is the only economically feasible way to go. By listing the anticipated objections and presenting them with answers, the presenter can address known resistance or disagreements and diffuse a potentially hostile situation.

Goals/Status. This is another updating or informing type of presentation. The goals may already be known to your audience, or you may be presenting them for the first time. Either way, this can be very informative or very motivating.

This is very common when companies meet to create or update their strategic plans. If a company has a multi-year strategic plan, listing the goals and updating each one is a logical format.

Exception Report. An exception report is typically a routine presentation or regular update. It highlights only the areas that are not normal in a larger context. This is often used in financial reporting. This can be useful for informing, but not necessarily for entertaining.

This method can be used in finance subcommittees or they may be used at a board of directors level. This method normally requires that financial reports be part of the presentation or handouts and the exceptions are either highlighted on the reports themselves or are made the subject of various visual aids. This kind of presentation is usually characterized by large numbers of graphs, charts, tables, or spreadsheets.

Issues/Status. This is another form of updating that is similar to an exception report, but may be less detail oriented. This method highlights particular items in a larger context or acts as a follow up from previous meetings.

In a routine meeting of a nonprofit board of directors, this method may be preferable to a departmental or committee update presentation if the information is repetitive from meeting to meeting. By bringing up only things that are different from previous meetings or only information that needs attention, this method can make more efficient use of meeting time and prove to be more informative.

A summary of the different kinds of body structure and their general usefulness in presentations to achieve the purposes of informing, entertaining, motivating, and persuading are presented in the following table:

	Inform	Entertain	Motivate	Persuade
Chronological	Excellent	Fair	Fair	Poor
Spatial	Excellent	Fair	Fair	Fair
Geographic	Excellent	Poor	Fair	Poor
Features/Benefits	Excellent	Fair	Excellent	Excellent
Compare/Contrast	Good	Fair	Good	Good
Numerical	Fair	Fair	Poor	Poor
Question/Answer	Good	Good	Good	Good
Departmental	Fair	Poor	Poor	Poor
Problem/Solution	Fair	Fair	Excellent	Excellent
General to Specific	Fair	Good	Excellent	Excellent
Objections/Answers	Excellent	Poor	Good	Good
Goals/Status	Excellent	Good	Excellent	Good
Exception Report	Fair	Poor	Fair	Fair
Issues/Status	Fair	Poor	Fair	Fair

Sometimes you may find that your information requires a combination of the structures covered here. No matter which structure or combination of structures you use, the structure should be uniform through the body of the presentation so that it is easy to follow. For example, you may be using the question and answer method, but one of the answers may have five enumerated answers.

The groups you identified in the brainstorming step should represent the individual items in whichever method you are using. So, if your groups from the brainstorming step ended up centering on geographic areas, each group of the body of your presentation will be a geographic location.

It is vitally important to remember that no matter what method you use, all of the items in the body of the presentation should support or prove your purpose. For example, if you use compare and contrast as your method, all of the comparison points would drive home your purpose of convincing the members of the audience why they should pick your product over the alternate.

In another example, if you use the chronological method, all of the points you make should have relevance to how you got to the present. Many chronological presentations have details that are irrelevant to the purpose. So in a chronological presentation, decision points or significant events work better to move the story along than a straight narrative.

Moving a presentation along brings us to the use of effective transitions. Just as ligaments hold bones together, effective transitions hold the points of a great presentation together. That is the subject of our next critical step.

Critical Step 6: Use smooth transitions

Once you determine your body structure, you will need a way to get your listeners through your ideas as in the illustration that follows:

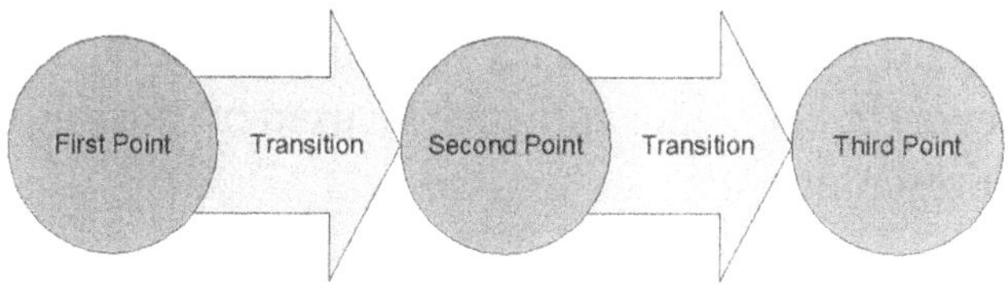

Transitions

Have you ever been reading a book and flipped back a few pages to check a name or fact that you read earlier? Or have you ever been watching a recorded movie and pushed rewind to hear a character repeat a line? A presentation is different. You must keep the members of the audience engaged and carry them through your presentation without losing them. They need to know where they are in your presentation and they certainly need to know when you have moved from one point to the next.

Transitions between points or concepts should be consistent so that your listeners know the transitions are upon them. They also need to be clear so that you don't end up in the next point and your listeners don't realize it. I have sat in a presentation when the presenter said, "...and the fourth reason we need to...." Before I heard that, I did not even realize there were three others.

Some main body structures have transitions built into them, but other structures will require more planning. You can certainly use transitions such as, "The next point I want to make is..." or "The fifth reason to buy or product is..." throughout your presentation and you will get through the information. However, in doing so, you are missing out on a great way to keep your audience focused on the purpose of the presentation.

There are several ways to use transitions smoothly and effectively. Some of the most effective ways are described below.

Tactic: Refer to your structure

Several structures make it easy to transition from point to point. For example, a numerical structure has transitions by default. A timeline in a chronological structure lets the listeners know where they are. Other types of structures may be more difficult, though. A general to specific structure or a spatial structure may require one or more of the transitions below.

Tactic: Ensure the audience is engaged

Checking in with the audience at transition points can make sure everyone is keeping up with you. You can keep the audience interested by reminding them what is in it for them. An effective way to do this is to ask a question at the end of a point you have just made. Some examples are:

- Why is this important to you?
- Why am I telling you this?
- How does this relate to our purpose here?

These questions can be turned into statements as well:

- This is important to you because…
- I am telling you this because…
- Another consideration regarding (state your purpose)…

Letting the audience catch up is particularly important if your presentation will be long. If you will be speaking for more than an hour, you will want to check in with your audience frequently to ensure they don't mentally check out on you.

Tactic: Ask clarifying questions

If your audience is not too large and if your presentation permits, you can ensure your listeners are engaged by asking catch up questions such as:

- Do you have any questions on this point?
- Is everyone with me?
- Can everyone see the importance of this point?

Ensure that this kind of check in questioning does not turn into a question and answer session. The purpose is simply to let the audience consider the point you just made. This method is effective when used with the following tactic.

Tactic: Use extended pauses

Let the audience catch up between major points in your presentation by pausing. You can do this effectively by taking a drink of water between each point or by walking slowly to another part of the room if you are standing. If you ask a clarifying question such as, "Is everyone with me?" you will need to give the listeners a chance to engage.

Pauses are very effective in many types of presentations, but beginning speakers often rush the pause or overestimate the length of an effective pause. If you have asked a clarifying question, a good measure is to count to ten slowly to yourself. This might seem like an eternity to less experienced speakers, especially ones that tend to talk quickly. Pauses during narration for dramatic effect can be shorter than a count to ten.

Tactic: Use structures of speech to transition

There are several ways to use language for transitions.

- *Alliteration.* This is where several things begin with the same letter. Example: the four cornerstones of responsible development are: Protecting the environment, Preserving open space, Providing for infrastructure, and Planning for schools.
- *Anaphora.* This is the same beginning to several different points. Example: Martin Luther King Jr. effectively repeats "I have a dream…" to make his points.
- *Epistrophe.* This is when the end of each point or sentence is the same. Example: "The planning *was perfect.* The preparation *was perfect.* The practice *was perfect.* The performance *was perfect.*" (This is a combination with alliteration.)
- *Tricolon.* This is using groupings of three. Threes are very effective because they carry excellent cadence and they are easy to follow. Example: A presentation may have three main points or it may have five main points and three subheadings under each point.

Using these kinds of language tools as transitions are less obvious than other ways of transitioning, but they are often used by advanced speakers. We will look at some other advanced tactics in Part Two of this book.

Tactic: Ask a rhetorical question

Asking a rhetorical question is a very effective transition tool. The question can tie a point just made to the point that follows. Here are some examples:

- Here is our production plan. Now, how are we going to sell the product? Here's how…
- That's how we got here today. Where are we going now? Pay attention…
- That's our plan. Who will be responsible for carrying it out? Here is the team…
- So all of the parts are in place. When do we start? I'll let Jim tell you…
- Now you know the story. What's left? We need your help with…

This tactic makes both points relevant to one another and creates an understanding of how your points fit together. The rhetorical question can also come at the end of the body of your presentation to act as a check in and to reinforce your main purpose as in the following example: "So what do these five things mean to you? Let me tell you." This brings you right back to the reason your listeners are there.

Tactic: Use consistency in transitions

No matter what kind of transitions you use in your presentation, try to make the transitions from point to point consistent. Once you use the second transition, you will have trained the audience to listen for your transitions. This will make them more effective and the audience will be able to keep up.

One time I listened to a speaker for about an hour and he had about ten transitions. Every single one was different. This was not by design; he had just not considered how transitions affected his presentation and he had evidently not practiced them. After the first few points in his speech, the transitions actually became a detractor, because I had to listen harder to know the transitions were upon me. Don't make this mistake unknowingly. Plan your transitions and make them easy to follow.

Critical Step 7: Create a dynamite opening

If the purpose of your speech is its heart, the main points are the bones, and the transitions are the ligaments, then the introduction and conclusion can be considered the muscles. Strong muscles make a strong body, and a strong opening will make your presentation very powerful. We will cover the purposes and kinds of openings in this chapter.

An audience will start making judgments about you even before you begin speaking. The audience may read or hear prepared remarks by someone else introducing you that will set a certain level of expectation. The listeners will hear your first few words and they will start processing verbal and nonverbal clues even before they understand what you are saying. Their impression of what you say and how you say it will determine their initial willingness to believe your message.

The opening of your speech serves several purposes. They are:

Grab the attention of the audience. The chances are you will be presenting to busy people with a lot on their minds. If you are in a series of presenters or if you are buried in an agenda, you will need to get your listeners to focus on you and you message. If your opening is weak, it will be difficult to recover. If you lose them in the first few sentences, or never actually grab their attention, their minds will start to wander right away.

Establish interest in your presentation. Your introduction or opening should give the audience a reason to listen to the rest of your presentation. If your listeners can't figure out why they should be listening in the very beginning, they won't listen.

Introduce your main purpose. Part of your planning (Critical Step 3) was to determine what value you offer your listeners. You want to let them know you have something of value for them early in your presentation. Ensure that by the end of your introduction the audience has a clear understanding of where you are going.

The simplified method of giving a speech that has been handed down through the years applies here:

- Tell them what you are going to tell them
- Tell them
- Tell them what you told them

But, of course, there is more to it than this to give a great presentation. Yes, the introduction serves to tell the audience where you are going, but it serves other purposes as well.

Establish credibility. You may be able to grab their attention, establish interest, and introduce your purpose, but why should they listen to you rather than someone else? You can use your introduction to establish credibility in a number of ways:

- Create a connection with the audience
- Give the audience a reason to like you
- Build rapport with credentials
- Show how you are like the listeners
- Show how you understand them

Your presentation stands a great chance of success if you can get the audience listening and believing you from the start.

Tactic: Warm them up with "Pre-Opener"

A pre-opener is the few words you say before you dive into your attention grabbing, purpose filled introduction. A pre-opener may only be a sentence or two. It should not be mistaken for your introduction. Think of the pre-opener as a transition into your introduction. There are several kinds of pre-openers:

Thank your introducer. If you are introduced, you will certainly want to thank the person introducing you. If this person is known to you, you can let your audience know that you have known the introducer for years to help establish credibility. In any event, compliment the introducer in some way.

Establish a link to the location. If you traveled to give your presentation, you might start by saying, "The first time I was here in Goshen, Indiana I met a very nice lady at the.... I am glad to be back." This helps establish a connection.

Briefly mention some current event. This is easy during any given sports seasons. "How 'bout them Cowboys/Redskins, Yankees/Red Sox, etc." If the location has a successful sports team, this helps build rapport with the audience (even if they cheer for another team).

Refer to something earlier on the agenda. If there are several other presentations or if you immediately follow someone else, you can tie into the previous speaker, especially if he or she was well received. If you can speak knowledgeably about other items on the agenda, you can build credibility.

Express your enthusiasm. This is perhaps my favorite pre-opening. You might say something like "I am really excited to be here because..." or "I love coming here because..." or "This is my favorite group/event/meeting because...." Statements like these let the audience know you are enthusiastic about what you are about to present, and as you know, enthusiasm is contagious.

Tactic: Grab them with an awesome opener

There are an infinite number of ways to open, but here are the most common:

Pose a question. This is a popular way to open and it can be very effective at getting the attention of the audience. The question could have an obvious answer, such as "How many people here brush their teeth every day?" Or it could be a little more variable, such as, "How long has it been since you changed the oil in your car?" Or it could be a little more personal, such as, "What is the most you ever paid for a pair of shoes?" The potential questions are endless. However, if you start with a question, make it relevant to your purpose. Even better, make the purpose of your presentation the answer to your question.

State a fact or statistic. This is a very good way to grab the attention of the audience, especially if the fact is revealing or outrageous. As with posing a question, the fact or statistic should help you get to your purpose. An example is, "The percentage of tax returns changed as the result of an audit is 96%. Our procedures are much easier to understand." The fact or statistic could be from your own material. For example, you might start with "Last month we signed our 15,000th customer."

Offer a quote. Famous or not famous, it doesn't matter, as long as it is applicable to your purpose. Worn out quotes are uninspiring, even if they were very inspiring when they were given. Avoid long quotes since you may lose the audience. Use care when reading a quote any time, but especially if it is your opening. This is where you want to win the audience's attention for the rest of the presentation. Don't blow it by messing up on the quote. Sometimes a very old quote from ancient Greece or Rome can be effective, especially of you can show how it is still applicable to your purpose today.

Tell an anecdote or short story. This can be a very effective opening if it is done well. Story telling is an art by itself, so this may require some practice. Starting with a story will also give you a good way to close your presentation. Be careful with the amount of time allotted to the story. Sometimes we feel the need to add detail when retelling a story, so the story might grow in length over time. Remember, the story is the introduction and should not become the presentation. As with all the other openers, the story should have relevance to your purpose.

Look to the past. This could be similar to stating a fact or statistic. It is useful for describing the progress of an organization. For example, you might say, "Five years ago we had five employees and one product. Today we have...." Or, "In 1993, we had a dream to.... Today we have realized that dream." These are simple, but very effective openings.

Use an analogy, simile, or metaphor. Many people get these three words mixed up or use them interchangeably. Therefore, some quick definitions follow:

- *An analogy* is stating a relationship between two things that don't appear to have anything in common. An example is "As iron is eaten by rust, so the envious are eaten by their own passion" (Antisthenes).

- *A simile* uses the words "like" or "as" in creating a relationship between two things. An example is "Teaching school is like having jumper cables hooked to your brain, draining all of the juice out of you" (Stephen King).
- *A metaphor* states that one thing *is* another. An example is "All the world's a stage, and all the men and women merely players" (Shakespeare).

These tools can be very effective at grabbing attention. You can use one of the millions already written, which would be starting off with a quote, or you can create your own. Some people can do it naturally. A friend of mine draws relationships between concepts often and regularly uses similes and analogies to get his ideas across. He makes them up on the spot, but they are very effective for him to get his point across.

Promise an outcome. "Before you leave here you will be convinced that…" or "By the time we are finished here, you will have learned how to juggle…" are both stating the intended outcome of the presentation. Promising an outcome is clear, and it states the purpose of the speech at the very beginning.

Declare your purpose. I recently heard a presentation that started out like this:

> *"I am here to talk with you about a very disturbing topic: teenage suicide. I will tell you what to look for,*

what to do, and where to go for help. I know these things now. My son took his life two years ago."

This was a very powerful opening to what was clearly going to be an informative speech. The speaker started out very directly by telling the listeners the exact purpose right at the beginning. Declaring your purpose can grab the audience's attention, establish interest, and establish credibility all at the same time.

Set the scene. Setting the scene often has the feel of a story associated with it. Here is a great example:

"January 17, 1991, 0400 hours. I was on the flight deck of the USS Theodore Roosevelt sitting in an F-14. It was pitch black out except for the flashlights of the deck crew. It was the first night of the Persian Gulf War. I was finishing up my pre-launch checklist, about to go into battle for the first time...."

Setting the scene as an opener transitions into the body well if the speech has a chronological structure to it.

Use a combination. You may find that a combination of openers is appropriate. For example:

"Thirty years ago, five percent of our school aged children were obese. [Look to the past and state a statistic.] Today, 40% are obese. We have a plan to reduce this by one third in the next ten years. [Statement of purpose.] In order to do this, we are going to need help. Will you help us?" [Pose a question or issue a challenge.]

Here is the opening to a speech by Susan B. Anthony defending herself in 1873. It is a combination of stating a fact, declaring a purpose, and promising an outcome:

> *Friends and fellow citizens: I stand before you tonight under indictment for the alleged crime of having voted at the last presidential election, without having the lawful right to vote. It shall be my work this evening to prove to you in thus voting, I not only committed no crime, but, instead, simply exercised my citizen's rights, guaranteed to me and all United States citizens by the National Constitution, beyond the power of any State to deny.*

Tactic: Don't open with a joke

Remember the four purposes of the introduction:

- Grab the audience's attention
- Establish interest in your topic
- Introduce your purpose
- Establish credibility

Telling a joke at the beginning of a presentation is dangerous. A joke may grab their attention, but it will do little else to help your presentation. Think about it: is the purpose of your introduction (or your presentation) to make people laugh at you? If you must tell a joke, ensure that your joke is applicable to your subject and that it will effectively transition your introduction into your body. Practice it well and make sure it is funny to everyone you try it on. Otherwise, use one of the other openers.

Tactic: Open with energy

Plan for your opening to have 80-85% of the maximum amount of energy or interest level that your presentation will have. If you start out at 100%, you have nowhere to go but down. Make sure you are at 100% for your closing.

Critical Step 8: Be smart with visual aids

If the purpose of your speech is its heart, the main points are the bones, the transitions are the ligaments, and the introduction provides muscular power, the visual aids can be considered the clothing of your presentation. This chapter will cover the construction of visual aids. We will discuss how to deliver the information in the visual aids in Part Two of this book.

Before we begin our discussion on visual aids, it is important to realize that visual aids are a rather recent development in the history of speeches and presentations. Keep in mind that virtually all of the best speeches in history were given without visual aids.

- Patrick Henry did not need them in his speech "Give me liberty or give me death!"
- Sojourner Truth did not use them for her "Ain't I a woman?" speech
- Franklin Roosevelt did not need them for his "Four Freedoms" speech in the Great Depression
- John F. Kennedy did not have slides at his inaugural address to make his point "Ask not what your country can do for you, ask what you can do for your country"

- Ronald Reagan did not have a multimedia clip to augment his "Tear down this wall" speech

Granted, these are examples of political speeches, and political speeches rarely have visual aids. But that is the point. The information in political speeches is no more or less complex than the information in your presentation.

At the other end of the spectrum, I was at a meeting not too long ago when the presenter told me before his speech that he had 110 slides to get through in about ten minutes. At first, I thought he was kidding, but he did accomplish this feat by the end of his speech. I don't remember what his speech was about, but I remember he had 110 slides.

If you are going to use visual aids in your presentation, consider the following tactics:

Tactic: Know the purpose of visual aids

It is important to know why you want to use visual aids. There are several purposes for using them:

To AID your presentation. The important word here is *aid.* This might sound obvious at first, but far too many presentations have been given where the visual aids *are* the presentation. Remember, you are the presenter, not the narrator. The visual aids should help you deliver the information. If they deliver all of the information, the audience doesn't need you. They can get the information in a handout or in an email.

To aid comprehension. There is no doubt that visual aids help your listeners absorb and understand your information better. Different people learn and assimilate information better in some ways than in others. Some like to hear it. Some like to see it. Others like to calculate it. Good visual aids will offer a variety of ways for your audience to acquire your message. In order to ensure you get the maximum penetration you can, you may want to include a variety of slides that include bullets, pictures, graphs, or other kinds of aids.

To clarify information. Visual aids will help your audience understand where you are in your presentation. They can help your audience see the big picture. The aids can also help the audience understand complicated or detailed information. Visual aids are helpful if you need to demonstrate:

- A spatial relationship between items
- A proportional relationship between items
- A chronological order

To add or keep interest. Visual aids can keep an audience engaged by reminding them where they are in the timeline of your presentation. If you set out in your opener that you have five things that you will cover in your presentation, the audience can visually see that you are near the end of point four. Also, the aids may put information in a context that your listeners had not considered before. This is particularly true with graphs and charts.

To keep the presentation on track. Having prepared visual aids should replace your notes when you give a presentation if you know your material well enough. The order will stay the same as you intended and you will stay on track, even if you forget where you are or if you get side tracked by a question or comment from the audience. Reminder: Do not read your visual aids to the audience. Your aids are not a transcript of your speech or presentation.

Tactic: Understand the requirements of visual aids

Before using any visual aid or even any slide, ask yourself the following questions:

- Is it necessary?
- Is it relevant?
- Is it informative?
- Is it worth it?
- Is it fool proof?

If you answer "No" to any of the above questions, don't use it.

Tactic: Recognize common problems with visual aids

Before creating your visual aids, it is helpful to know what not to do first. The most common visual aids are presentation slides on a screen, so that is what we will focus on here. In order to help you recognize some of the most common problems with slides, consider the following slide:

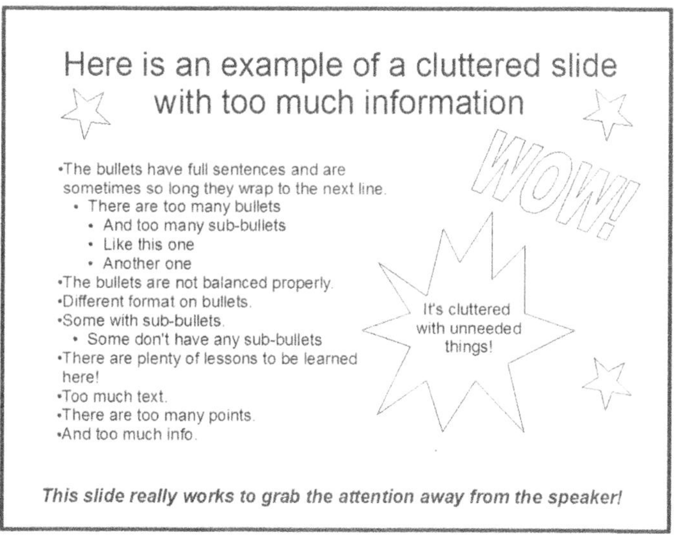

Example of a cluttered slide

This slide has some problems that many slides have. They are:

Too hard to read. This can be a range of problems, but the main problem with readability is the size of the font. The size of the room will determine the smallest font size you can use, but anything smaller than 24 font is getting pretty small for a presentation slide. Color and contrast also play a part in readability. High contrast between letters and background works best. Some people prefer light on dark for certain circumstances and dark on light for others, but the idea here is to maintain high contrast. The rule to remember is the person sitting farthest away from the screen should be able to read it.

Too cluttered. Modern software makes it easy to add all sorts of information, add-ins, add-ons, clip art, imbedded items, shapes, charts, etc. The more things that are on a slide, the harder it is to read and the more it will take away from your presentation. Also, if there are too many things on a slide, the audience will focus on the slide and not on you. If the audience has to process a dozen or more items on the slide, they may not hear you at all.

Too much data. How many points are you trying to make with one slide? If you have too much data, it will be cluttered *and* hard to read. If you want to include all of the information, break it into two slides. Better yet, edit it down and fill in the gaps as part of your presentation. Remember, the slides are there to aid your presentation, not deliver it. Symptoms of this are too many bullets or too many sub-bullets. A good rule to follow is a 6 x 6 configuration. Don't have more than six bullets on a slide or six words per bullet.

Unbalanced bullets. Effective treatment of bulleted items is often overlooked. For example, all the bullets in a list should be balanced. This means that they should all start with nouns or all start with verbs and the verbs should be in the same tense.

The guidelines governing outlining generally apply to bulleting as well. For example, a point should not have one sub-point. If it only has one sub-point, the sub-point should be moved up a level. The purpose of sub-points is to create sub-lists and a list is more than one.

There are other common problems with slides, such as:

Not relevant/not applicable. Have you ever been in a presentation where the presenter put up a slide and either began talking about something else or started talking about the slide and wandered off to another subject? Or have you ever seen anyone put up a slide and then either skip it or say it is not important or that they won't be covering that? It happens all the time. A variation of this is when the presenter puts up a very busy or cluttered slide and only discusses a small portion of it and moves on. This leaves the audience wondering what they missed.

The slides are documents. This is a common mistake. This happens often in financial meetings when the presenter puts financial statements on the screen. It could also happen in a board of directors meeting if the presenter puts up the annual report or the strategic plan and this happens frequently in state and local government meetings when the presenter puts a law or ordinance on the screen.

Sometimes the members of the audience have the documents in front of them as handouts and the presenter reads while they follow along. In cases like this, the document is becoming the presentation. Your presentation can *interpret the document, summarize the document, or evaluate the document,* but if you find yourself reading a document, someone in the audience is likely thinking, "I can read it myself, thanks."

Tactic: Create great visual aids

We have covered the purposes of visual aids, the requirements for visual aids, and some problems with visual aids. You may start out thinking that creating slides for a presentation is a daunting task. Fortunately, if you follow the steps and tactics up to this point and create your presentation first, creating the visual aids should be much easier than sitting down and trying to create a presentation from the visual aids.

The method you chose to carry your audience through the main body of your presentation will help you format your slides. For example, if your presentation is the question and answer format simply put each question on its own slide and discuss the answer as you give your presentation. You can insert supporting slides in between questions. The same goes for an issues/answer format or a problem/solution format.

Here are some additional considerations in creating your visual aids:

Ensure your slides are readable. The slides must be readable for all members of your audience. This includes appropriate font size and letter/background contrast. The most effective way to ensure readability is to set the presentation up in the room in which you will give it, and ensure you can see it from all angles. If you cannot visit the room prior to your presentation, a size 24 is the probably the smallest size font you should use in preparing the slides.

Provide a mixture of slide types. Avoid repeating the same slide type over and over. Since different people prefer assimilating material in different ways, avoiding a repetitious presentation will increase your chances of keeping everyone interested and involved. Also, twenty bullet slides in a row will start to get monotonous. Twenty bar charts in a row will make the audience restless. Mix it up to keep it interesting.

Declutter the slides as much as possible. This applies to all kinds of slide whether they are bullet slides, charts, graphs, or other kinds of slides. The slide is too cluttered if the audience has to try to figure out the main point of the slide.

- Limit each slide to one major point
- Ensure text slides are balanced
- Use consistent phrasing in bulleted lists
- Use upper and lower case letters
- Consider revealing bullets individually

Don't get carried away with slide transitions. Fades and dissolves, wipes, pushes and covers, stripes and bars, etc. are all ways to handle slide transitions. I remember many years ago when I first saw slide transitions used.

The speaker used a different one for each transition and the audience began to "oooh and aaah" (mockingly) every time the speaker advanced the slides. In this situation, the transitions took attention away from the points the speaker was trying to convey. The lesson here: don't let the features drown out the message.

Tactic: Using other kinds of visual aids

Presentation software is making it easier every day to create great looking presentations. It is now easier than ever to imbed video and internet links into your presentation. It is beyond the scope of this book to get into the fine points of creating video presentations. Bear in mind, however, that more is not always better. There is probably a reason you have been asked to give the presentation. If technology allows you to let the presentation take center stage and you become the emcee, you can probably just email the presentation to your group and wait by your phone for questions.

This chapter on visual aids has focused on creating visual aids with presentation software such as Microsoft PowerPoint, Open Office Draw, or other programs. Other kinds of visual aids, such as using a white board, flip charts, and handouts are covered in Part Two of this book because their use has more to do with technique rather than construction. But the questions to consider when using visual aids still apply to any kind of visual aid.

Critical Step 9: Add dimension

If the visual aids are the clothing of your presentation, the tactics in this chapter are the accessories. Once you have the introduction, the body, and the visual aids for your presentation, you can go back and dress it up to make it even more interesting, more memorable, and more powerful.

The following are the most common ways to add dimension to your presentation:

Use meaningful examples. The first time we see something, we make judgments about it based on what we see at the time combined with what we have already experienced in life up to that point. In a room full of people that do not have common backgrounds it is helpful to point out something that they may all have knowledge about so they can then make the comparison to the concept you are presenting at that moment. In this manner, you are in control of the comparison. Otherwise, your audience members will use their own examples inside their own heads to compare to your concept.

For example, if you are trying to convey the feeling of what it was like when your company merged with another company, you could compare it to the same feelings you had the day you got married (if the majority of the your audience is married). You could express the happiness you felt along with the recognition of big changes ahead.

Examples also help the audience to understand how the concept you are presenting applies to them. Remember, you must keep your presentation focused on what you have to offer your audience.

Use descriptive stories. Stories can make a presentation come alive. When telling a story, try to involve as many of the senses as possible to engage the audience. Include sights, sounds, smells, temperatures, and anything else that can add to the experience.

When telling a story, make sure it has a purpose that supports your main purpose. As when telling a story in your introduction, ensure that the story takes only its proportional amount of time. If your presentation is 20 minutes, make sure your story doesn't take a majority of your time.

Recall a known emotion, feeling, or sense. This can be a very powerful way to connect with your audience. If you are trying to get them to imagine something, bring it to life, such as in the following examples:

- "It's like that feeling you get when you suddenly realize you are running through a red light."
- "You know that feeling in your stomach when you are at the top of the roller coaster and you start to head straight down?"

- "Have you ever opened a container of sour milk?

Use quotations with care. Quotations are easy to come by and can help you demonstrate your points. As with any other aid, ensure the quote is relevant. Avoid long quotes and avoid using too many quotes.

Use statistics and facts. Statistics and facts can be useful for making your presentation come alive. They can be used to help you make your points clear and measurable. If you use statistics and facts, ensure they are verifiable, and that they can't be easily turned around. For example, passing test scores may have dropped, but maybe the grading system changed. Avoid ambiguous statements such as "It is a well known fact that…" or "Research shows that…" or "Scientists say…." If you are going to cite a fact or statistic, cite the source at the time of delivery.

Use interactivity. It is often a good idea to get interactive with an audience if your presentation goes for more than about 45 minutes. Straight lecture for longer than this can induce even the most attentive listeners' thoughts to wander.

Some ideas for interaction are:

- Ask the audience to guess the answer to something
- Ask questions to individuals in the audience
- Recruit volunteers to help

- Get the audience to share examples or experiences
- Break the audience into work groups

Anything you do to get the audience out of "receive" mode will help keep everyone engaged.

Use analogies, similes, and metaphors. We covered these in Critical Step 7 when we discussed openings. They can also be used very effectively throughout your presentation. They can be a theme of your subject, or they can be used individually.

Use structured speech. We discussed some structures of speech in Critical Step 6 when we looked at effective transitions. Using structured speech such as alliteration, anaphora, epistrophe, and tricolon can also help make your speech sound great. Certain kinds of structures have been used for centuries, but they sometimes get lost in translations. However, they have been used effectively in American speeches since Colonial times. In his First Inaugural Address, Thomas Jefferson used the tricolon:

> *"...peace, commerce, and honest friendship with all nations..."*

Jefferson also used anaphora with the tricolon:

> *"...freedom of religion, freedom of the press, and freedom of person...."*

President Obama has used structured speech extensively. Consider this passage from his inaugural address on January 20, 2009:

> *For us, they packed up their few worldly possessions and travelled across oceans in search of a new life.*
> *For us, they toiled in sweatshops and settled the West; endured the lash of the whip; and plowed the hard earth.*
> *For us, they fought and died, in places like Concord and Gettysburg; Normandy and Khe Sahn.*

This passage employs the anaphora by repeating "For us…." He uses the tricolon with three points and embeds another tricolon in the second phrase. When listening to this passage, his emphasis rises and falls with each phrase.

Later in that same speech he offered the following:

> *Recall that earlier generations faced down fascism and communism not just with missiles and tanks, but with sturdy alliances and enduring convictions. They understood that our power alone cannot protect us, nor does it entitle us to do as we please. Instead, they knew that our power grows through its prudent use; our security emanates from the justness of our cause, the force of our example, the tempering qualities of humility and restraint.*

This paragraph is very structured. It has three sentences. Two are balanced sentences followed by a third employing another tricolon. Read this aloud and you can feel the rhythm.

When adding dimension to your presentation with the methods above, don't just sprinkle them throughout your presentation. Ask the same questions that you did for your visual aids in determining whether to use them or not:

- Is it necessary?
- Is it relevant?
- Is it informative?
- Is it worth it?
- Is it fool proof?

Critical Step 10: Conclude with strength

As with your opening, you want to close as strongly as possible. The audience should understand and remember your main purpose, and you want your listeners to remember your purpose after your presentation. If you follow the critical steps in this book, the closing will be much easier to plan and execute than if you don't. The important word here is *plan*. If you carefully craft your body and meticulously prepare your opening, you can still leave your listeners thinking they missed something if you just drift off with "Thank you" or "That's all I've got."

Your opening and closing are your two most important times in your presentation. We covered earlier that the opening should be at 80-85% of the energy level and interest level of your presentation. The closing should be at 100%.

The purpose of your closing should be to drive home the purpose of your presentation. To prepare your closing, keep the following in mind:

Tactic: Indicate or signal your intent to close

If you indicate your intent to close, the audience will mentally close the door on getting new information and look to you to finish achieving your purpose of informing, entertaining, motivating, or persuading. The listeners become tuned in to your final comments. Be sure to take advantage of this when you transition to close. Here are a few ways to indicate your intent to close:

- Use transition phrasing such as, "I'll end with…" or "Here's a final thought…" or "Before I leave…" or "Now, here's what we've covered…" or "My purpose here today is…"
- Put a summary slide on the screen
- Use an extended pause
- Refer to your opening, such as "Remember the quote…"

Tactic: Let your structure help you close

If you used a question/answer format, you can start your closing by saying that you have covered five of the most common questions about your topic. Whether you repeat your questions or not is a matter of timing and preference. If you used the compare/contrast format, you can say, "I have demonstrated the differences…."

Tactic: Make your closing complement your opening

One of the purposes of the opening of your presentation is to inform the audience of your purpose. You closing should ensure that you achieved your purpose. If you started by posing a question, show how you answered it. If you started with a fact or statistic, show how you plan to change it. If you started with a quote, show how the quote applies now that you have made your point. If you started with a story, tell the end of the story.

Closing with something your listeners are already familiar with is a method of teaching or reinforcing something they have already been exposed to. Even most comedians giving a monologue with seemingly random information will close with a reference to something earlier in their performance. Closing with a reference to your opening puts bookends at both ends of your presentation and holds them together.

Tactic: Leave them with something more

What is the takeaway of your presentation? Remember, if you can get the audience to recall your purpose a week later, you have made great progress. In order to leave your audience with something to remember, consider the following:

- Tell a success story demonstrating your purpose
- Show how your proposal can influence the future
- Issue a challenge to the audience
- Declare the next steps or make a call to action

All of these methods are ways to drive home your purpose and increase the retention of your message.

Tactic: Avoid these common killer mistakes in closing

A poor closing can kill a great presentation. You may have planned a great closing and you may even have executed it well, but you can still blow it by making one of these common mistakes:

Apologizing. Don't apologize at the end of your speech. Don't apologize for the room or your cough or the weather or for speaking too long (see below). The closing is not the time to apologize. If you feel you must apologize for something, do it at some other time.

Adding a new concept. Don't try to add information at the close. If you transitioned to the closing effectively, your audience already mentally closed the door on new information coming in.

Trying to cover something missed. This is combines the first two mistakes and makes the situation worse. You will find yourself apologizing for not covering the material and then you will be trying to add new information. Remember, the audience does not know that you missed something, so don't bring it up.

Speaking past the high point. Suppose you made a great presentation and you had a terrific closing. Stop talking. Don't go past the 100% energy point. If you made your point, declared your call to action, or issued your challenge, stop there.

Thanking the audience. This is a little more stylistic than the other mistakes, but it has its importance. A speaker ordinarily should not thank the audience. What is the purpose? Is it to thank the audience for listening? The audience should thank the speaker under most circumstances, except perhaps if the speaker is accepting an award. The difference may seem small, but if the speaker thanks the audience, it is as if the speaker has taken time away from the listeners and is thanking them for that time. A "Thank you for taking the time to listen" close can subtly dilute an otherwise powerful closing.

Not having an exit plan. What are you going to do as soon as you close? What will you say? The most common thing to do here is to have a positive hand off back to the host, moderator, or emcee. It could be as simple as saying the person's name and looking at him or her. If the format does not permit this or you did not receive an introduction, you may need to introduce the next person. Be prepared for this and have the introduction ready. No matter what the situation, remember that you have just led a room full of people through your presentation. You want to introduce them to their next leader or you lead them to their next destination. This is courteous and professional, and it lets your listeners know you have not abandoned them.

Summary of Part One

We have looked at the critical steps to planning and preparing a great speech or presentation. If you follow the steps in order, you are well on your way to delivering the best performance that you can. The steps are:

Planning Phase:

Critical Step 1: Have a plan before you begin
Critical Step 2: Establish your purpose
Critical Step 3: Determine "What's in it for them?"
Critical Step 4: Brainstorm

Preparation Phase:

Critical Step 5: Determine your structure
Critical Step 6: Use smooth transitions
Critical Step 7: Create a dynamite opening
Critical Step 8: Be smart with visual aids
Critical Step 9: Add dimension
Critical Step 10: Conclude with strength

If you have gone through these ten Critical Steps, you are ready to move to the next phase, the Practicing Phase. We will cover this in detail in Part Two of this book.

Part Two:

Perform Like a Professional

The Practicing Phase

Part One of this book deals with planning and preparing your speech. If you do the Critical Steps presented in the order they are given, you will have assembled the parts and materials to make a great presentation. Part Two of this book will show you how to polish your presentation.

The Strategies presented in Part Two are all about delivery. They can be applied to your presentation in any order. The more of them you incorporate into your presentation, the more polished and professional your presentation will become. The Strategies in Part Two are filled with tactics. Don't be worried if you cannot get all of the tactics at first. You may find, like I have found, that it is very difficult to focus on all of them at the same time. Work on some and move on to others.

You will discover that the more you practice your presentation, the easier it will be to incorporate more of the tactics into your presentation. The reason for this is that the better you know certain parts of your presentation, the less you have to worry about them. You can then allocate more time and effort into incorporating additional tactics into your plan. As with anything, the more you practice, the better you will get.

Strategy: Reduce nervousness

Glossophobia is the fear of public speaking. It is most likely linked to other fears, such as fear of failure or fear of rejection. Fear of public speaking is unlike fear of spiders, snakes or heights. A bite from a spider or snake or a fall from a high place, while unlikely, could harm someone. There are very few cases of anyone actually dying or being harmed from giving a speech or presentation.

Nonetheless, most speakers must deal with some fear or anxiety. It is natural and is to be expected. The only way to get rid of most of the anxiety may be to speak in public regularly or give the same presentation over and over. I say "most" because even professional speakers get butterflies. I have a theory that the adrenaline rush you get before presenting is one reason some people actually *like* speaking in public.

So how can we deal with the butterflies? Here are some great ways:

Tactic: Be totally prepared

If you are as prepared as you can be, then you will be a long way toward reducing nervousness. Some books on public speaking have dealing with nervousness at or near their beginnings. This subject is located after the planning and preparation phases in this book because the thought "What if I mess up?" will be greatly reduced if you have planned and prepared properly and adequately. If you have planned and prepared through the Critical Steps in Part One of this book, you will have eliminated virtually all of the things that can go wrong. I have seen thousands of presentations. Some were very bad. However, I can say that just about all of the poor presentations I have seen are linked to poor planning and preparation.

Tactic: Focus on the audience

One reason the fear exists is because it is self focused. Anxiety about what might happen or what might go wrong can overwhelm the thoughts of a presenter. One way to reduce the fear is to focus on the audience. Do you think the audience is scared about your speech? That is doubtful. Focus on ensuring the audience gets what they want and need and you will have less reason to focus on yourself. Ask yourself the following kinds of questions:

- Will my purpose be clear to them?
- Will they get my main points? How can I be sure?
- Do my examples relate to the audience?
- What will make them remember the presentation or cause them to take action?

If you keep audience focused, your anxiety level will go down.

Tactic: Write down your fears

Let's think this through for a moment. What is the worst thing that can happen to you? That you will freeze up? That you will be rejected? That you will fail—whatever that means? Try to write these fears down. All of them. Once you make a list of them, write down why you have the fear next to each one. Find the source of each fear. You may find that once you write them down they will look much less intimidating. You may begin to see some or most of them as they really are: irrelevant.

Tactic: Forget your anxiety

Sometimes knowing when your fear will end helps you deal with it. If your speech is more than just a few minutes long, the chances are that your fear will be gone a few minutes into it. Most people forget about their fears after the first few sentences. Once you see some receptive faces and you realize you won't die, you will be able to focus on your material better. By the time you are into the body of your speech and moving toward your closing, you will likely have forgotten all about your anxieties.

Tactic: Know your opening perfectly

Since you will likely begin to forget your fear sometime after your introduction, be completely familiar with your opening. If it is short, it is not unreasonable to have it memorized. This way you can be assured you will get through your opening without any of your worst fears happening.

Tactic: Recognize that they can't see your legs shaking

Most people in your audience won't be able to tell you are nervous. I have been in countless presentations where the speaker confided in me afterward that he or she was very nervous while they were speaking. The reality is that I could not tell if the person was nervous if he or she had not told me. So there is a key lesson in here: don't start your presentation by telling everyone how nervous you are. Just smile and no one will know but you.

Tactic: Find friends in the audience

One of the reasons that speaking in front of an audience is different from a conversation with one or two people is the lack of two way communication. When you are speaking to a group, they are not necessarily giving you the kind of feedback you are accustomed to. One of your fears may be that you don't know how they will react while you are talking, and this can be very intimidating. If you are able to meet some of the people in your audience before your presentation, find them and look them in the eye while you are speaking. They will likely give you some sort of feedback such as a head nod, a smile, or an approving look. This positive feedback can help you get the feedback you are used to while you are speaking.

Tactic: Remember to breathe

When I first started speaking in front of groups, I found that I would inhale more than I was exhaling. This would result in my lungs being fuller and fuller as I tried to speak. The cure to this was to slow down my speaking and to take a few pauses and deep breaths. In a state of anxiety, it is sometimes difficult to exhale. Remember to breathe deeply just before you present to help you relax. But just as importantly, remember to pause and breathe deeply after you begin speaking.

Strategy: Practice, practice, practice

Back in Critical Step 1, we found that you should plan on allocating 25% of the time you have to get ready for your presentation to practicing. You may be tempted to skip or reduce this step, but the more effort you put into practicing, the better your presentation will be. Here are a few things to consider when practicing:

Tactic: Practice out loud

Don't believe that practicing in your head or saying the words to yourself will actually work. You cannot practice by reading your material. It simply won't work. You will not get the words, transitions, or timing right. No amount of reading your material will take the place of saying your words out loud.

Tactic: Use a mirror

You might think this is silly, but it works. Talk to the mirror as you practice your presentation. You will see your facial expressions and notice where you need to add gestures. Practice looking yourself in the eye.

Tactic: Record yourself

If you can record your voice, you will learn much about your speaking. Record yourself as you practice your presentation and pay particular attention to the following:

- Are you emphasizing the points the way you want to?
- Is your energy level where you want it at certain times of the presentation?
- Are your transitions smooth and natural?
- Are you using pauses effectively?
- Do you have excessive "crutch" words, such as "uh," "um," "you know," and "like?"

You may be surprised at what you hear.

If you are able to video record yourself, you will learn even more. Most courses on public speaking include video recordings of the participants. In the courses I have taught, the participants are often very enlightened when they see themselves giving their presentations. If you record yourself, make the recording session a dress rehearsal as close to the real thing as possible, including using the visual aids. Take note of the following:

- Do your facial expressions match your intended enthusiasm?
- Are your gestures appropriate? Can you see them?

- Do you have any physical distracters such as scratching your nose or flipping your hair?
- Are you talking to the visual aids instead of the audience?
- Are you staring at your notes?

These are all things that can be revealed if you see yourself on video prior to giving your presentation.

Tactic: Practice in front of others

If it is practical, perform your presentation for someone else and have them evaluate you. Have them do the following:

- Write down everything they see, both good and bad
- Tell you what they like the most about your presentation
- Let you know what they think you need to work on most (this is often not the same thing you think you need to work on)
- Say if they got the main purpose
- Determine if they could follow the structure
- See if they can remember your main points
- Point out where you need emphasis
- Evaluate your opening
- See if your examples are effective
- Comment on your transitions
- Assess your closing
- Count your "crutch words"

You will find this kind of feedback invaluable to you while you are practicing your presentation.

Tactic: Use time wisely

Timing your presentation is very important. Effective use of time is a result of good planning, preparation, and practice. In most cases you will know how long you have to give your presentation. If you don't have a set time that is determined by your circumstances, set one for yourself so that you can practice toward a consistent time.

Do an initial run through your presentation covering all the points you want to cover without stopping and check the time. Assess if you need to cut anything out or if you need to expand on some points. In my experience in observing presentations with time issues, probably 90% or more run long. Very few speeches are too short. Speakers who run long may lose their audiences prior to their closings, particularly if they run past their allotted time or a scheduled break.

Once you have run through your material a few times, create time markers in your presentation, so you know where you are. For example, if you have practiced enough to know that your second point is halfway through your material, make a note to do a time check there to make sure you do not run long and have to rush your finish. Be sure to set a time point at the beginning of your closing so you know you have enough time to finish.

Time yourself every time you practice. Recognize that the more you practice, the more your timing can change. For example, as you practice, you may find that you need to expand on a particular point to make it clear or that a story needs more detail to make it effective. The last few times you practice, your delivery should not change much, so your timing should be accurate.

Strategy: Set the tone

Setting the tone of your speech is critical to an effective delivery. It begins as you are being introduced and goes well into your opening. By that time, the audience has already begun to decide, intentionally or otherwise, whether to accept your message or not.

Imagine the following scenario:

> *A speaker comes to the lectern who has his shoulders slumped, who is looking down, and is beginning to shuffle his notes as he approaches. He apologizes for not being ready. He says he is sorry, but the room is too bright to be able to see his slides well. He puts his pile of notes on the lectern and looks down at them. He never makes eye contact with the audience. He begins to read his notes with, "The first thing I want to tell you is…."*

Obviously this speaker is off to a bad start. Here are some tactics to help you set the best tone possible for your presentation:

Tactic: Meet and greet the audience

Whenever possible, meet the members of your audience ahead of time. If you are presenting to a group of investors, a group of politicians, or a group of association members, try to meet as many of them as possible prior to the presentation. This will help you identify people in the audience that you can relate to (see Strategy: Reduce nervousness). This will also give the members of the audience the feeling that they already know you.

Tactic: Have your host read your introduction

If you have someone introducing you, prepare a written introduction for that person to read *verbatim* to the audience. Do not assume that this person knows what to say or knows how to say it. You eliminate a potential awkward situation if you know what is going to be said as you are walking up. The person introducing you will appreciate not having to ad lib your introduction. Give the person the introduction typed in very large font, double spaced, so that he or she can read it very easily.

Tactic: Start on time

If you do not have someone introducing you, be sure to start on time. This is important in gaining control of the audience. If the audience believes you are in control, they are more likely to give you their attention. Starting on time may require giving a five minute warning to start. Many people in the audience will appreciate your punctuality and respect for their time.

Tactic: Approach with confidence

Shake hands with your introducer if you have one. Then approach the podium (the one that goes to the floor) or lectern (the one that sits on top of a table) calmly and with confidence. This means have your shoulders back and your head up, looking at the audience. Smile. Get eye contact with several of your listeners, especially if you met them before your presentation. Look at them and acknowledge that you see them with a head nod, additional smile, or eyebrow raise.

Tactic: Use your eyes to open theirs

You open a great speech with eye contact. Many people get to the lectern or podium and look down at their notes and begin reading. This is a crucial time to draw the audience in by establishing eye contact. If you lose the audience early, it is hard to get them back.

During the rest of your presentation, maintain eye contact by shifting your gaze from person to person. Don't focus on one individual or one section of the room for the entire presentation. Some people always talk to the back of the room, but this can alienate those closer in. Make broad sweeps with your eyes, stop on an individual for two to three seconds, and move on.

Tactic: Start with enthusiasm

Radiate to the audience that you are glad to be there. Remember, the audience is there to hear what you have to say. Unless you are delivering bad news or are at a funeral, demonstrate to the audience that you are excited to be there. Your energy level will transfer to the audience and get you listeners in a receptive mode. If they know you are excited about your subject, they will want to share in your excitement.

Keep in mind that you want to start off your presentation at about 80-85% of your maximum energy level. You will want to finish at 100%.

Tactic: Thank the introducer and address the audience

This may seem obvious at first, but the thank you serves two purposes. It acknowledges the person introducing you, and it acts as a natural transition.

Once you have thanked your introducer, it is customary to address or acknowledge members of your audience. This is often done in order of seniority. At a military event, the tradition is to address the chain of command individually. This could take quite a while. There is often a flourish by a band for each of the highest ranking officers. In a political environment, this could mean introducing elected officials in order of their offices. You would address a U.S. senator, then a U.S. representative, then the governor, the mayor, the council members, etc. In a business environment, the CEO would be addressed first, and so on. You may elect not to address everyone in order, but it is almost always appropriate to thank your introducer and the highest ranking individual in the room.

Tactic: Don't apologize

Starting out with an apology is starting out weak. If your apology is something beyond your control, your audience will understand. If you have a scratchy throat, don't apologize to everyone for being sick. Mental shields will automatically go up to avoid germs—and your message. Do what you can to compensate. If you feel you must draw attention to your voice or health, try to incorporate it into your introduction. For example, you might say, "The last time my voice was this hoarse, I was cheering our victory at achieving our goals. Let's hope we have the same result this time."

Tactic: Don't complain

If there is something wrong with your environment, such as noise coming from an adjacent room or if the lighting is not right, do what you can to address it. If you can't, then compensate for it the best you can, but don't start off with a complaint. Some people tune out right away if someone starts out complaining.

Tactic: Stop on time

Don't go over your allotted time. If you are scheduled to stop before a break, stop on time or your audience will start to check out. Stopping on time shows discipline and it shows respect for others' time. If you get started late due to no fault of your own, ask to have the agenda adjusted, if possible, to give you your full time. If this cannot be done, assess the amount of time you have and adjust your presentation accordingly. Do not complain if you get shorted on time. This happens very frequently and you need to be prepared to give your presentation in different amounts of time.

Setting the right tone before and during your presentation can make a large difference in the way your message is received. Pay attention to the tone you set using the tactics above to make your best possible presentation.

Strategy: Deal with distractors

Distractors are the things that speakers do that take the listeners' attention away from the speaker's message. People will do the strangest things when they get in front of a group of people. Sometimes these things are caused by nervousness, sometimes they are habits that tend to show up more on the podium or at the lectern.

The best way to be aware of your distractors is to practice your presentation in front of someone who will be honest with you. You can also see your distractors if you have a video recording of yourself.

Sometimes even the best speakers have distractors. I recently attended an event that is put on quarterly by an economic forecaster. He had been giving the same type of presentation four times a year for the past fifteen years or so. He had a habit of sniffing and then wiping his nose. I thought at first he might have had a cold. I saw him at another event and he did the same thing. I met him afterward and he had no signs of a cold.

When I was in the Navy taking a course on officer protocol and conduct (we called it knife and fork school), the woman who was giving the course wore half-rim glasses. Her glasses tended to slip down her nose every few minutes. After she spoke for quite some time we all began to watch her glasses as they slipped, waiting to see how far down her nose they would go. The tension would build as her glassed traveled down her bridge. When they reached the *very* end of her nose, she would push them back up and the entire class would breathe a big sigh of relief and relax. I can still remember this presenter's distractor even though it happened more than twenty years ago.

Here is a list of common distractors. We all tend to have one or more. Sometimes it seems that once we conquer one, another one crops up. If you have any of them, perhaps someone you know or someone you practice with will point them out to you.

- Jingling change in your pocket
- Strumming your fingers
- Playing with or clicking a pen
- Leaning on the podium or lectern
- Nervous cough
- Flipping or curling hair
- Stuffing your hands in your pockets
- Crossing your arms
- Twirling your glasses
- Scratching, rubbing, or picking your nose
- Tugging on your ear
- Chewing on things, such as the ends of pens
- Biting your lips
- Continuously clearing your throat
- Stroking your mustache or beard
- Rubbing the back of your neck
- Tapping your feet

- Bouncing on your toes
- Twisting a ring or playing with jewelry
- Standing on one foot
- Rocking back and forth
- Twisting your body
- Backing up from podium or lectern

Identifying a distractor will get you well on your way to eliminating it. Once you become aware of it, you will probably be able to drop it with a little practice.

Strategy: Sharpen your speech

Once you have started speaking, the way you say your words will have an impact on the way your message is received. The following tactics will help you sharpen your delivery.

Tactic: Reduce or eliminate "crutch" words

Crutch words are filler words in our spoken language. Words such as "ah," "um," you know," "actually," and many others are very common. Even professional speakers and radio or talk show hosts fall prey to them.

The best way to know if you are using any crutch words is to record yourself. If you record yourself practicing your presentation, you should be able to hear your own crutch words. Even after you listen to yourself, you may not recognize less obvious crutch words. For example, some people may start off many sentences with the word "see" or "so" without noticing it, even if they hear it recorded. Therefore, getting someone to listen to your speech to point out any crutch words will help you identify them. Knowing that you have one or more crutch words gets you well on your way to reducing them. I recently pointed out a crutch word to someone who had no idea he was using it. Once he became aware that he was using it, he was able to start reducing its occurrence.

Once you identify a crutch word, stop yourself each time you hear yourself say it and start over. If you have someone listening to you practice your presentation, try having that person say your crutch word out loud every time you say it or signaling you somehow each time you use it. Some speech classes have the instructor sound a clicker or other noise maker every time the speaker says a crutch word.

Becoming aware of your crutch words gets you well underway to eliminating them.

Tactic: Over-enunciate for clarity

Speaking with one or two people is different than speaking in front of a group, just as speaking in front of a group is different than speaking in front of a large audience. The larger your audience, the clearer your enunciation needs to be. Perhaps the most common enunciation problem is curtailing the "-ing" at the ends of words. Words such as "saying," "changing," and "trying" come out as "sayin'," "changin'," and "tryin'." Over-enunciating these words sounds like this: "saying-ah," "changing-ah," and "trying-ah."

Some radio personalities, such as Paul Harvey, over-enunciate their words, especially the ends of words. For example, saying "words" very clearly sounds like "words-ah." Zig Ziglar has very clear diction and is famous for "over-enunciating-ah" his "words-ah."

Another way to help your enunciation is to over-exaggerate your facial movements while talking. Stage performers learn this as part of their training. It is hard not to enunciate clearly if you are over-exaggerating your facial expressions.

Other examples of enunciation problems are using improper contractions such as "gonna" and "shoulda." Avoid multiple contraction words. My friend often says to me "jyeetyet?" which means "did you eat yet?"

The more you can clarify your words, the better you will be understood. Clarifying your words and sharpening your delivery will also give you the distinct advantage of becoming more credible. Clipping your words and using improper contractions will make your speech more casual, which often has the effect of making it less believable and less authoritative. Unless you're tryin' to soun' like Jeff Foxworthy, enunciate clearly for greater effectiveness.

Tactic: Use short sentences

The spoken word is not like the written word. As we covered in Critical Step 6, your listeners do not have the advantage of rewinding you if they don't follow your sentences. Speak clearly and speak concisely. Powerful speakers have known this for centuries. Consider Patrick Henry's conclusion to his most famous speech:

> *It is in vain, sir, to extenuate the matter. Gentlemen may cry, "Peace! Peace!" but there is no peace. The*

war is actually begun! The next gale that sweeps from the north will bring to our ears the clash of resounding arms! Our brethren are already in the field! Why stand we here idle? What is it that gentlemen wish? What would they have? If life so dear, or peace so sweet, as to be purchased at the price of slavery? Forbid it, Almighty God! I know not what course others may take; but as for me, give me liberty or give me death!

Tactic: Avoid jargon and acronyms

My best friend from childhood and I both went to Aviation Officer Candidate School in Pensacola, Florida. I remember one Christmas break after we had both been commissioned as navy ensigns. We had dinner at his family's home and we spoke to one another using words that must have seemed like a foreign language to his family. The military is notorious for its acronyms and jargon that is difficult or impossible for anyone else to understand.

The same can be true in the civilian world. Unless you are speaking in front of a homogeneous group of engineers, software designers, chemists, or other specialized group, speak to those that may not know your specialized language. Spell out acronyms on slides, and don't assume everyone knows what you are talking about.

Tactic: Avoid worn out parts of speech

If you are going to use descriptive language, use something other than old, worn out phrases such as:

- Square peg in a round hole
- Sharp as a tack
- 800 pound gorilla
- Busy as a bee
- Let the cat out of the bag
- Hard as a rock
- Egg on your face

If you are going to spend time preparing your presentation, you might as well use phrases that really sparkle and shine. If you are going to try to describe something, try using an uncommon phrase, come up with an original description, or even try coining your own phrase. For example, my friend from Texas is fond of saying, "I've already been to this rodeo" which has a greater impact than, "Been there, done that." You don't hear his comment every day, but you know what it means and it is very descriptive.

Strategy: Use vocal variety for maximum impact

Using vocal variety can yield perhaps the greatest return on investment of any speaking skills. Vocal variety can change a dull and boring presentation into an interesting and exciting one. Sometimes the material makes it easy to modulate your voice, sometimes it doesn't. For example, it is almost impossible to read a Dr. Seuss book out loud without using significant voice inflection. On the other hand, it is challenging to read a long list of statistics with considerable variability.

Several ways to use vocal variety to enhance your presentation are as follows:

Tactic: Use voice speed for emphasis

Your speaking speed, or pace, can greatly influence your message. When you are approaching an exciting part of your presentation, picking up speed will get the audience paying closer attention, especially of your speed picks up sharply. This is especially useful if you have incorporated a story into your presentation. If there is an exciting part of the story or if there is an action scene in your story, you can pick up the pace to bring it to life.

Slowing down from your normal pace has the same effect. If you want to make a specific point, you can slow... your...speed...down. Your listeners will pay closer attention. Draw them in by slowing down dramatically and maintaining eye contact for maximum effect. Speak slower to make points or add an element of drama, but be sure to resume speed so you don't lose your audience.

Tactic: Use voice volume to add emphasis

Volume and speed are often interconnected. If you increase your speed dramatically, you may also increase your volume at the same time. If you are describing a battle scene, you would likely pick up both speed and volume.

You can use volume in other ways, too. For example, instead of saying, "and then we decided to do point number 2," you could say, "and then 'BAM!' It HIT us that doing point 2 was the OBVIOUS DECISION!" This transition into talking about point 2 will be much greater and you will have the attention of the audience because it sounds like something exciting is coming.

A higher voice volume adds credibility to your message. A raised volume can convey to the audience that you have confidence and a good command of the information you are presenting. A weaker or softer voice can do just the opposite.

You can intentionally reduce your volume for effect as well. If you go down to a whisper that you know everyone will hear and understand, you will get your listeners to pay close attention. Even something as simple as whispering, "Let me tell you a secret" will draw your audience in closer.

Advanced speakers can alter the ebb and flow of their speech speed and volume like waves crashing and receding on a beach to keep the audience engaged.

Tactic: Use pauses for dramatic effect

Occasional or infrequent speakers often find making well placed pauses difficult. They are often so intent on getting through the information that they either forget to pause or don't pause long enough. A five second pause can feel like a five minute pause. You may have pauses planned onto your presentation, but even if you use them they may feel way too long. Pauses are effective in the following kinds of situations:

- At the transition from major point to major point
- After a rhetorical question
- At a dramatic fact
- At a decision point
- After a long quote
- After a significant voice speed or volume change
- Just before an important statement

You can use a dramatic pause anywhere your audience needs to catch up mentally or think about what you have just said. Letting your audience assimilate what you have just said and then hitting them with an important or impactful statement multiplies the effect of a well placed pause.

Franklin Roosevelt used this tactic effectively with a three-count pause in his first inaugural address on March 4, 1933, when he said, "So, first of all, let me assert my firm belief that the only thing we have to fear, [pause] is fear itself…."

On June 12, 1887, at the Brandenburg Gate in West Germany, Ronald Reagan had a very dramatic pause planned in his speech when he said, "Come here to this gate! Mr. Gorbachev, open this gate! [Long pause.] Mr. Gorbachev, tear down this wall!"

Strategy: Use your body as a visual aid

Your gestures can either add or subtract from your presentation. We covered many things not to do in the Strategy: Dealing with distractors. What you do with your body, arms, and hands when they are not distracting the audience is very important.

Tactic: Use your hands for emphasis

Your hands should rest comfortably on the lectern or podium during your presentation if they are not gesturing to add to your presentation. Don't put your hands in your pockets, behind your back, or in front of you in a "fig leaf" fashion.

Some people talk naturally with their hands in motion. This is fine for your presentation as long as they don't turn into distractors. Having something planned for your hands and arms to do during your presentation will help you control them from doing something unconsciously. For example, think of anything in your presentation that implies spatial orientation. If you say that something increases or decreases, goes up or down, or goes forward or backward (even in time) use your arms to imply the direction. If you are describing any kind of movement, use your arms and hands to demonstrate the movement. Look through your entire presentation to see if there is any place you can do this. Where you find these places, mark them in your notes to remember to make the movements at the appropriate times.

Tactic: Move around to keep your audience engaged

If you will be speaking for more than about 20 minutes, you may consider walking around the room to keep your audience focused on you. Beginning speakers may be too intimidated to do this, but it is very effective for longer presentations.

You can move around even for shorter presentations. I saw this done very well by someone giving a presentation where he recalled being in a large room at church where people had taped papers to the wall with prayers on them. As he described the scene, he walked away from the lectern and began to walk around the room, telling us about the prayers taped to the wall as if they were actually there. This was a remarkably effective way to convey his message, while keeping us all completely engaged.

I have seen people stand on chairs or tables, dance, juggle, and use many other methods of moving around to make their message memorable. Remember Jack Palance's one armed push-ups at the 64th Annual Academy Awards in 1992? He won Best Supporting Actor for his role as Curly in *City Slickers*. Remember who won in 1993? I don't either.

Strategy: Use notes wisely

There are several ways to keep you on track in your presentation. We will cover the following methods: use an outline or bullet format; write a manuscript; memorize your speech; or speak from your visual aids.

Tactic: Speak from an outline or bulleted notes

This is the preferred method of using notes. If you have followed the Critical Steps in Part 1 of this book, putting your notes together in outline or bulleted form should not be a problem. You can put the main points on cards or on a single piece of paper with a few bullets under each main point to remind you of your sequence and keep you on track.

Using outline or bulleted notes have several advantages. They:

- Are easy to follow
- Dissuade you from looking down and focusing on them
- Allow you to talk in a conversational tone
- Give you freedom to maneuver physically and verbally
- Let you expand, contract, or change your speech if needed

When preparing notes in this manner, here are some guidelines to follow:

Memorize your introduction. We covered a variety of opening options in Critical Step 7 in Part One of this book. Starting out your presentation exactly as you have practiced it will help you start the way you expect and help alleviate nervousness you might have. Refrain from reading your introduction verbatim from your notes.

Leave space in your notes. Leave space between points or put one point per card. This will make it easier to find your place if you if you get lost in your delivery. Trying to find your place in your notes is hard to do when you are on the podium or lectern. One person says it is like getting tunnel vision when trying to find your place.

Number the cards or pages. It is amazing how often notes can get mixed up during a speech or presentation. They can get out of order at the lectern or if you drop them, they can get shuffled.

Memorize your closing. Don't read your closing. If you don't memorize it word for word, at least know it well enough not to have to reference your notes. If it is too long to know it without reference, it is probably too long.

Tactic: Don't read your speech

Do your best not to read a manuscript of what you want to say. Remember, written sentences are often longer and more complex than spoken ones. Your audience cannot push a rewind button to go back over a point they did not get or to find the verb in a very long sentence.

There are several downsides to reading your presentation:

- It significantly limits your eye contact with the audience
- It increases the chance of making you lose your place
- It increases the chance of misapplying proper or intended emphasis
- It increases the chance of losing the audience
- You can come across as less confident
- It limits your gestures and body movements
- It ties you to the podium or lectern
- It makes vocal variety difficult
- It makes changing or adapting to the audience or situation very difficult
- You could just email or send it to your audience

You may occasionally find that reading your information is warranted. This may be in a press conference or public relations scenario where you will be quoted. It may also be in a legal situation where you want to sure you say exactly what you want to say word for word. Typically, written statements are short, and are not really presentations. In these kinds of cases, it is helpful to consider the following when preparing your script:

- Use large font
- Double or triple space lines
- Use bold headings
- Designate pauses or emphasis points
- Do anything to overcome the downsides listed above

Tactic: Memorize your entire speech with care

Sometimes for a short speech or presentation it makes sense to memorize the whole thing. You could memorize it word for word, as in memorizing poetry, or you could memorize your main points and speak naturally as you go through your presentation. This can be a very effective way to present, but it will likely require more practice than the other methods to ensure you can do it without forgetting something or losing your place.

Tactic: Use visual aids as your notes

The previous three ways of presenting—with outline or bulleted notes, with a manuscript, or memorized—can all be used if you do not have visual aids. If your presentation will have visual aids, you probably won't need notes if you use the aids effectively.

In Critical Step 8 in Part 1 of this book we covered ways to create great visual aids for your presentation. If you use visual aids from the beginning to the end of your presentation, you should be able to proceed through your presentation using the aids as your notes.

If you did not or do not prepare your own visual aids, you must know the material well enough to move through the information. If you find you cannot get through a presentation with visual aids without needing additional notes, you probably don't know the material well.

The next strategy covers tips and tactics to consider when using visual aids.

Strategy: Use visual aids like a professional speaker

In Critical Step 8 in Part One of this book, we covered *how to create* your visual aids. This section covers *how to use* them. We will assume that you have already created your great slide show or visual aids and that you are preparing to give your presentation.

The following are tactics to help you make your presentation polished and professional.

Tactic: Know when to turn your visual aids on and off

Some books on public speaking will tell you never to turn on your projector until you are ready. I agree with this to an extent. I do believe, however, that it is appropriate to have a title screen with your name and the name of your speech or presentation on it before you begin speaking. Many people are not great with names, and they may benefit from having your name on the screen as they are assessing you. I do agree that you do not want to introduce any other slides until you are ready.

Be aware of what is on the screen at all times. I recall giving a speech one time where my final slide was my name and speech title. The projector remained on and the host came up directly after me and introduced the next speaker. My slide was still up with my name and speech title on it. I exited and it was a few minutes until I came back into the room. I looked up and saw my slide still up there several minutes into the next person's speech. I had to track down the event coordinator to get the situation corrected.

A corollary to knowing when to turn on the projector is knowing when to turn it off. If you have segments of your speech where you are covering material that is not supported by a visual aid, turn the projector off so that you are not talking about something different than what is on the screen.

Finally, remember to turn off your computer's screen saver for your presentation. This is just another distraction you don't need, especially if your screen saver is picture of your child with spaghetti on her head.

Tactic: Stand to the left of the screen

People read from left to right. They will be looking at you on the left of the screen and their eyes will move to the right as new information appears on the screen. If you are on the right side of the screen when new information comes up, the audience will be going backwards.

This is not to say that you cannot move around and stop on the left of the screen on occasion. Just make an attempt to be at the left of the screen when new information comes up.

Tactic: Talk to the audience, not the screen

This may seem obvious, but judging by the number of people who talk to the screen, it may not be as obvious as it should be. If you need to look at the screen, look at it, and then look at the audience before speaking.

If you followed the tactic of standing to the left of the screen, point with your left hand so that you are open to the audience. If you point with your right hand or arm, you will cross your own body and you will be facing the screen. This takes some practice, since most people are right handed and will want to point with their right hand. This might make you feel like Vanna White on *The Wheel of Fortune*, but that is the point.

Tactic: Present the visual, and then pause

You know what is coming next, but your audience does not. Don't be tempted to speak while your visual is coming up. The audience is reading your slide, so they are not listening to you anyway. Present the slide and let the information soak in before proceeding. This lets the audience move from listening to reading and back to listening again.

Tactic: Be wary of laser pointers

Laser pointers were the rage when they first came out. Some people are still very enamored with them. But they do have their downsides. They:

- Are distracting if the user continues underlining or circling something with it
- Shake with an unsteady hand, especially at longer distances
- Require facing the screen to use them
- Encourage speaking to the screen

If you prepare your slides or visual aids with the guidance in Part 1, (e.g., they are easy to read, uncluttered, etc.) you should be able to reference the points on your slides without using a pointer.

Tactic: Pace your slides

Don't skip slides that your audience can see. Remove them. If you skip over slides and say, "I don't have time for that," or "That's not important," the audience will think they are being shorted. If you have a slide in your presentation and it comes up for all to see, comment on it, even if you are running short on time.

The pacing of slides can affect your presentation. I once gave a day long seminar with a very knowledgeable instructor. He had a habit of putting on the first slide and talking for an hour and a half with the same slide showing. When it was time for a break, he would shuffle through the next several slides muttering, "...covered that...that's not important...don't need to see that one...." He blasted through perhaps twenty slides without stopping. I found this quite distracting, and I know the audience was frustrated.

Pace your presentation and get into a rhythm. An audience will appreciate that you keep moving and they won't feel bogged down in one area. If you do what the fellow did in the example above, the audience will feel like it is getting jerked by a chain. Lead them along predictably.

Tactic: Don't apologize for a slide

This is a very common mistake. I have heard this countless times.

- "I know you can't read this but…"
- "This is somewhat cluttered, but…"
- "Someone else prepared this slide, but…"
- "I know this looks like an eye chart, but…"

If you find yourself needing to say anything like this, change the slide or eliminate it. Similar to not apologizing in your introduction, don't apologize during your presentation. Fix it or don't use it.

Tactic: Use traditional visual aids

You may decide to use more traditional visual aids such as flip charts or a white board. Many of the tactics for computerized aids apply to traditional aids as well. For example:

- Ensure everyone can read them
- Don't talk to the flip chart or board

- Don't block them while you are talking

Some additional things to remember are:

- Ensure your handwriting is legible
- Use flipcharts with lined paper
- Ensure writing instruments are fresh
- Don't talk while writing

Here's a tip: if you know what you are going to write on the flip chart, write it lightly in pencil at the top corner of the page ahead of time where even people on the first row can't read it. Then you can reference your notes as you write large enough for the audience to see.

Strategy: Dazzle them with Q&A

Many fantastic presentations end with a question and answer session. Sometimes the Q&A session will be on the agenda and other times you will decide to make time for it in your presentation. Either way, if you do not handle the Q&A session well, it can kill an otherwise terrific speech.

The Q&A session is a time in the presentation that you do not have complete control over the material, so there is a danger that the presentation may head in an unflattering direction. However, the Q&A session can add credibility and help you finish off your presentation very strongly.

The following tactics will help you keep as much control of the situation as possible.

Tactic: Have a few questions ready

You may find that you open up the presentation for Q&A and nobody asks a question. The time people need to think of questions can seem infinitely longer than a planned pause. Don't feel the need to jump in right away. A good guideline is to count to ten slowly to allow listeners to think of questions. Of course, someone may jump right in and ask. But if they don't, and you have counted to ten, you don't want to close and be done. This may lead the audience to think that your presentation wasn't even worth following up with a question. Once you have opened for Q&A, you must keep going.

If nobody asks a question, have one ready and say something like, "After hearing this information, some people wonder if…" or "Often, people ask…." Using this method of priming the question pump may get the audience thinking of other questions.

An alternative method is to plant some questions in the audience. You can ask a friendly listener or colleague ahead of time to ask the first question to get the session moving. Either way of getting questions going will serve the same purpose. If nobody follows up, you can wait another ten seconds and then close.

Tactic: Control your Q&A time

You want to maintain control of the audience without losing credibility, so don't announce that you have ten minutes for questions or that you can answer a certain number of questions. You can say, "We have a little time left to cover any specific questions you might have." If the energy winds down or if nobody asks any questions (see above), move to your final closing.

Tactic: Thank the questioner

Be sure to thank the person asking the question and follow up with an acknowledgement. Your response might sound like this: "Thank you for asking. That is a great question" or "Thank you. I'm glad you brought that up." Use the Q&A time to build rapport with your audience.

Tactic: Ensure everyone can hear the question

This sounds simple, but many times a speaker will take a question and start to go into the answer when half the room doesn't hear the question. Repeat or restate the question if there is any doubt that anyone heard it. Thanking the questioner (above) and then repeating the question gives you time to reflect on the question and formulate your best response.

Tactic: Answer for everyone

This is a common trap that speakers fall into: someone asks a question specific to themselves or their situation which does not affect anyone else in the room, and the speaker goes on for several minutes addressing one person. Be aware that everyone wants to know how your information affects him or her. For example, if you are giving an informational presentation on a proposed departmental change and someone asks about how they are going to personally affected by new procedures, ensure that your answer is general enough to benefit everyone, not just the questioner.

The danger in answering someone's specific question is that you end up leaving the rest of the audience to daydream, talk, or start checking their messages. Expect questions like this in a Q&A session and either answer in a way that can benefit everyone or tell the person that you can meet afterward to discuss it off line.

Tactic: Stay focused in your answers

Sometimes a questioner will ask you something somewhat or totally unrelated to your presentation. If you decide to answer, try to make your answer support your original message. Use the Q&A session to reinforce points you already made in a slightly different way. This will add credibility to both you and your presentation.

If someone asks you a question that is obviously off message such as "Who's going to win the super bowl this year?" after your presentation on non-governmental organizations in Africa, don't answer because then everyone starts thinking about football. If that type of question comes toward the end of a Q&A session, that is your cue to wrap it up.

Tactic: Be aware of the attack question

Attack questions can come in several disguises. Your questioner might:

- Make a long statement of position followed by a challenge
- Make a false statement disguised as a question
- Ask a series of questions
- Make a hostile series of statements that don't appear to end

- Attempt to promote a position different from yours
- Bait you with a lose/lose choice

Under circumstances like this, someone is trying to take your presentation time and either make their own point or discredit yours. Being aware that this is happening is your greatest asset to defending against it. It is your presentation, so don't allow someone else to take over. Don't get defensive. There are several ways to combat the hostile question or attempted takeover:

- Restate the question in a friendly way, such as "If you mean what positive steps are we going to take to…"
- If there are multiple questions, say "You have asked a lot, but I can tell you this…"
- Discredit the questioner by saying, "I'm not sure where you got your data, but…"
- Acknowledge the attack and sidestep by saying, "That's one way of looking at it, but here's my point…"
- Interrupt the attacker and say "Hold on, thank you for pointing that out—I'll be glad to cover that off line…"

Tactic: Don't be afraid to say "I don't know"

Admitting you don't know the answer is better than trying to make something up on the spot. It is better to tell the questioner you can get the answer afterwards. You might also open it up to the audience and say, "I'm not sure, does anyone here know the answer?"

Tactic: Use Q&A time creatively

One time I was on a panel and the panel members were all told we would have a certain amount of time each to make some initial comments after which we would entertain some questions. As it turned out, one of the panel members used up more than his allotted time and my time was cut short. I made some brief comments and waited until the questions. As soon as I fielded my first question, I answered it quickly and went back into my presentation material and covered all of the points I wanted to make.

You can do this, too. If you forget something in your speech, don't tell the audience you forgot. If you get to the questions, you can offer the information you left out, but you can make it sound like bonus information. You might say, "The answer to your question is yes. You might recall that I gave you four reasons to consider our proposal. A fifth point might be…." This is a great way to recover, and the audience not only doesn't know you forgot something, they think they got something extra.

Tactic: Have a second closing ready after Q&A

At the conclusion of Q&A, don't just say "Thank you" and hand it back to the host. In the Q&A session, you do not have control of the content, so you don't want to leave the lectern or podium after a non-flattering question or one you don't know the answer to.

If you know you are going to answer questions, have two closings ready: one to give at the end of your presentation and one to give after the questions. Having your second closing ready to give after the last question will give the audience a better chance of remembering you and your message. No matter how you choose to close (see Critical Step 10 in Part 1 of this book), do it after the questions to leave your greatest impact.

Strategy: Speak like a professional

If you read Part One of this book and follow the ten Critical Steps to give a presentation, you can likely survive without being too embarrassed. If you follow the Strategies in Part Two of this book up to here, you will likely give a great presentation.

The following are a few advanced tactics and skills that I have learned over more than 20 years of speaking in front of groups. These advanced tactics will help you take your speaking abilities to the next level.

Tactic: Measure your presentation energy level

The energy level will naturally go up and down during a speech or presentation. Knowing where the energy level rises and falls will help you craft your words, actions, and aids to provide maximum effectiveness.

Consider the following assessment of energy through a presentation:

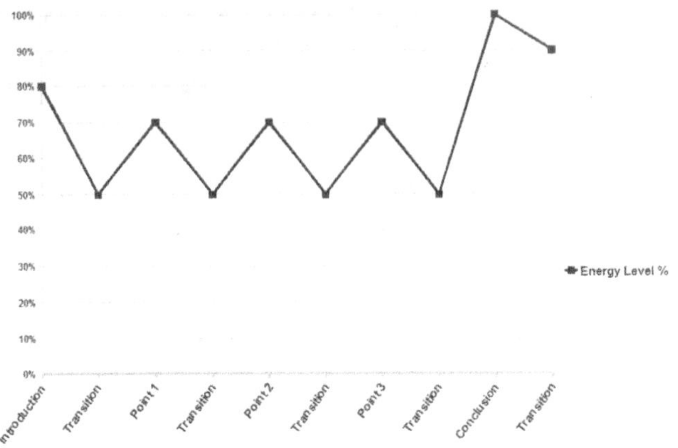

This is what you might expect the energy level of the audience to look like through your presentation. You grab attention with the opener, grab attention with each new point, and finish strong.

I have a story that I often tell to audiences about an experience in combat that has an energy reading like this:

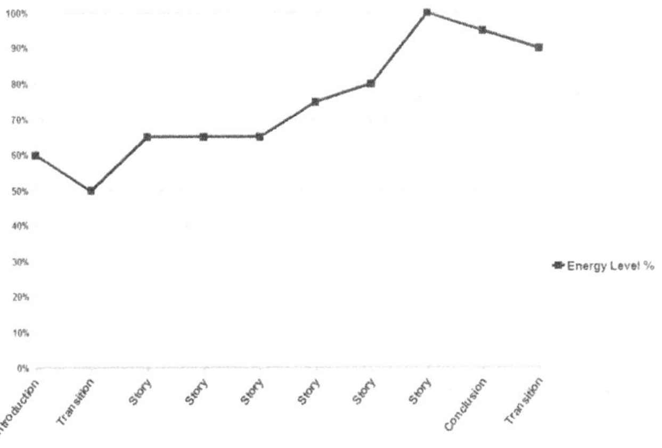

My story starts off with a somber attention grabber. I go into the narrative and people get comfortable with the scene I have set and they get accustomed to my voice. I slowly start to build energy and I consciously begin to increase my pace. My words get louder and my pace gets much faster as the story unfolds. I build it to a climax where the energy is at its maximum. I drop the volume and speed back down some at the very end after the battle, but the audience still has adrenaline flowing and quickly beating hearts (if I have done well).

If you start weak, say with a bad joke or an apology of some kind, recover slightly with point 1, but lose your audience from there, your energy graph might look like this:

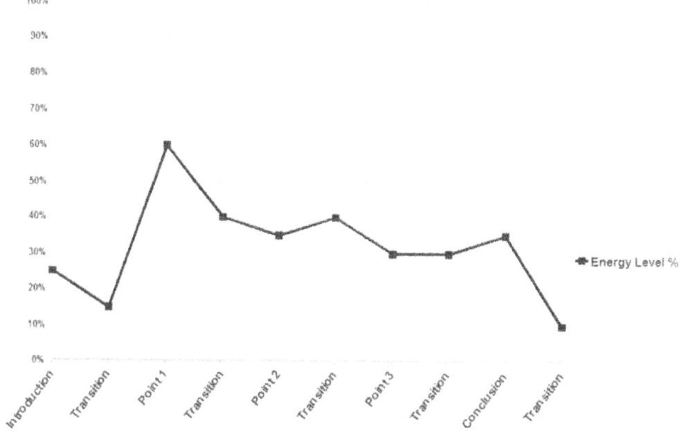

Look at your material, your aids, and your planned pauses and gestures, and determine what you think your graph might look like. Then get someone to listen to your presentation and assess it for you in the same way. If it looks like the third example, you will want to make some major changes.

Tactic: Prepare a condensed version

If you find yourself giving the same presentation to several groups, or if you will be one of many presenting in a given time slot, you will need to be flexible on time. You may have prepared for an hour presentation, but only get 15 minutes. If you find yourself short on time, you need to be able to give your presentation over a variety of time periods. If you know you will be short on time, ensure you condense material over your entire presentation. Don't start out at your rehearsed pace and speed through the second half.

One way to handle a short time situation is to know what slides you can delete ahead of time if you are using visual aids. As I stated earlier, don't skip slides (where the audience can see you skipping through them), but *remove* them instead. You can do this by having a separate file with a shortened version of your presentation in it, or you can hide the slides.

Another way to handle this is to show only your conclusion slide. You can make abbreviated comments on your main points and put up the final slide.

One thing that I have done for some longer presentations is to make the final section just before the conclusion an expandable and retractable section. This section might include a planned Q&A session, a work session, or an audience participation section. In several instances, I have put a bulleted list before the conclusion so that I could go over each one independently, or I could just say, "And here is a list of other things this subject applies to as well." This "accordion" technique can be a great asset if you are running long or short on time.

In any of the situations above, don't complain about the time, and don't apologize. If you get shorted on time, it is not your fault. Don't say things such as, "If I had more time…" because you don't. If anyone wants to hear more, they will find a way to hear what you have to say either by giving you more time or by contacting you afterward. Give your best possible presentation in the time you have.

Tactic: Find a spy or neutralize an enemy

This sounds more cutthroat than it is. Many times when you give a presentation you will be the most knowledgeable person in the room on the subject. Occasionally, however, someone else in the room may know much more about your subject than you do.

One time I was giving a very technical presentation on a missile delivery system and I knew there was someone in the audience that had been involved in the design and testing of the system. He had a reputation of being a bit of a know-it-all, and he had a habit of interrupting people and correcting them when they spoke about his areas of expertise. I sought him out ahead of time to go over my material, and at the beginning of the presentation, I pointed him out by name and told the audience that I had consulted him in the preparation of the material. During the presentation, I looked over at him (on the front row) and nodded at him as if to get approval on some of the points I was making. He had no choice but to be my ally. He did not interrupt and did not attempt to disrupt my presentation.

You can do the same thing for your presentation. If you know someone is potentially hostile, meet with that person ahead of time to get input and then acknowledge that person. It will diffuse a potential threat and add credibility at the same time.

A variation on this theme is to find an ally ahead of time and let her know you might ask her a question or ask if she will confirm a point for you. You might say, "Mary has done a lot of research on this point and can verify it. Right Mary?" This is part of the building rapport with the audience tactic as well.

Tactic: Acknowledge audience body language

Once you know your material and you are perfecting your delivery, begin to pay attention to your audience and how they are reacting to you and your message. This is something great presenters do very well. They are able to gauge how well the audience absorbed the last point they made and are able to tell if they need to back up and cover a point again. When giving your presentation, some signs to look for include:

- Talking
- Fidgeting
- Paper shuffling
- Quizzical looks
- Absent stares
- Texting or checking email
- Shaking heads
- Grumbling
- Sleeping

A novice speaker may continue on with a presentation in the presence of one or more of these, but a more experience speaker will pick up on these signals and adjust the presentation accordingly. For example, if you experience some quizzical looks, you might ask your audience if they have any questions, but they might not answer. They may not even know enough to ask a question. In this case, you might go over a point again or reinforce it with another example.

If you are losing your audience to boredom, distraction or inattention, you can try one of the following:

- Eliminate some detail
- Change your volume
- Change your pace
- Add to or change your body movement
- Ask the audience a question
- Take a survey or a vote
- Walk towards the wayward listeners
- Make a loud noise
- Say "Here's what you really need to know"

You can do many things, but the key here is to be aware of the attentiveness and interest level of your audience and be able to adjust if it is not where you want it or expect it to be.

Tactic: Handle mistakes with care

You may find two thirds the way through your presentation that you forgot something. If you have not made a critical error in your logic or in making your case, your audience probably won't know. You do not have to start apologizing or backing up. You may have presence of mind enough to be able to recover but you don't need to draw attention to it. By drawing attention to it, you will distract the audience and you may lose some credibility with regard to your knowledge of the subject.

If you have made an error in logic, or if you have left out a critical piece of information, you can reposition yourself and say something like this: "Before you can make a decision, most people would like to know this...."

Occasionally, you may forget where you are. You don't need to panic here. There are several things you can do:

- Pause, and think
- Ask a rhetorical question
- Take a drink of water
- Move a display or move around
- Ask if everyone is with you

- Ask if the temperature in the room is OK
- Ask "Where was I?

Your audience will help you if you ask them.

Strategy: Get ready for the big day

Once you have your presentation totally prepared and you have practiced all you can, find out as much about your venue as you can. If you are presenting locally, you will want to visit the site before giving your presentation. If you are traveling, you need to arrive in plenty of time to acclimate to the site and find out all you can. The more you know about your site, the better off you will be.

The following will help you be as prepared as possible with regard to knowing your environment:

Tactic: Arrive early to make adjustments

If you can, visit the site ahead of time, preferably a day or more in advance. This will allow you to make changes to your presentation if you need to. If you are traveling, get to your location as early as possible prior to your meeting. Most locations you will deal with will allow you to enter early to set up if you ask.

Allow yourself plenty of time for setup. You will want to set up your equipment and test it if you can. Arrange the tables if you are able to. If you are in a conference room, moving the tables may not be an option. However, you may find that someone set up the room in a classroom setup when you want a more face to face setup, such as having the tables arranged in a large rectangle. Don't be bashful about moving the tables around.

Tactic: Have a backup plan for everything

When I travel for a presentation, I bring my materials in several formats.

- Old and new software formats
- Copied onto CD, DVD, and flash drive
- In an email attachment
- PDF format
- Overhead slides
- Paper copies

This way, I can get to my material no matter what happens. I can give the presentation with no electrical power if I have to. If a plug doesn't work or a bulb burns out, I have a backup plan ready. I used to carry a spare overhead projector bulb when overheads were the primary visual aid delivery method.

Think through every possible thing that can go wrong. If you speak enough times, they will all happen eventually.

Tactic: Know where you are on the agenda

Are you presenting at 8:00 in the morning? Are you the first speaker after lunch? Are you the last speaker at a very long meeting? Knowing where you are on the agenda might make you want to make slight adjustments to your presentation.

For example, if you are scheduled right after a controversial matter that goes for two hours, you might call for a break. If you cannot get a break, you might ask your listeners to stand up and do five jumping jacks and shake hands with three people they don't know or something similar. This is like eating crackers between samplings at a wine tasting. You want to get the taste of the last thing gone before you start.

Time of day has implications, too. People are often fresh in the morning, lethargic after lunch, and in a hurry at 5:00 PM. You can adjust your presentation slightly to account for variations in your audience's energy level.

Tactic: Have a checklist of items

Here are some things you may want to check or have ready before your presentation. There may be others more specific to your presentation, but this is a starting point.

Meeting Room

- Room size
- Table setup (can you move them?)
- Visual obstacles (columns, glare, etc.)
- Lighting control location
- Electrical power (three prongs or two?)

- Internet access
- Window and door locations
- Temperature control location (accessible?)
- Lectern or podium (lighted?)

Equipment

- Microphone (test)
- Projector (test)
- Extension cords (three prongs or two?)
- Flip charts or white boards
- Markers (check each)
- Sound system (check)
- Remote controls (check all)
- Computer to projector plugs and cords
- Voice recorder

Supplies

- Note pads
- Writing instruments
- Handouts
- Tape
- Paper agenda
- Extra power cords
- Paper clips/rubber bands/tacks
- Markers
- Batteries for everything
- Refreshments
- Sugar (for diabetics)

Building

- Early access (Before hours? Will it be locked?)
- Copy machine availability
- Fire exits
- Parking (How far away? Cost involved?)
- Location of food facilities
- Location of rest rooms

These are some things to jog your memory. In addition to the list here, also think about your audience. Are you making a pitch to Microsoft using a Mac computer? Are you making a presentation to Pepsi and have Coke for refreshments? Are you instructing people on how to plan for the unexpected without having thought through the list here?

Strategy: Stay in speaking shape

Speaking in public is not something that comes naturally to many people. Nor is it like riding a bike or swimming that you can do well forever once you learn how to do it once. It is a "perishable" skill like many sports. For example, if you have not played a sport for several years that you once played often, it is unlikely that you can just pick up where you left off. Many golfers can relate to this. However, public speaking is a skill that can be improved upon and maintained with some attention and practice.

Speaking in public, like many things, gets easier the more you do it. The more you practice, the better you will get. So how do you practice? Here are some ways:

Tactic: Volunteer

This may sound crazy to you if you have anxiety about speaking, but seeking out opportunities to speak at work or in your personal life is not difficult. At work, you can volunteer to teach a class on something or inform your coworkers about something affecting your business. In your personal life, you can join a book club where you give a book report every so often. Pay attention every time you hear someone speak about something and ask yourself if you can volunteer to do the same thing.

Tactic: Join a civic group

Getting into a leadership position in an organization such as your homeowners' association, your Parent Teacher Association, or other civic group will give you the opportunity to practice speaking. Keep in mind that just by joining does not mean you will have the opportunity to speak. Many volunteers don't speak up in meetings and don't get to practice their speaking skills.

Tactic: Join a non-profit board of directors

Similar to volunteering for a civic organization, volunteering for a non-profit organization will give you plenty of opportunities to speak. You may make formal presentations or you may be on a board of directors where you speak more conversationally at meetings. Either way, you may be speaking in front of more people than you normally would otherwise.

Tactic: Volunteer to teach

This is a sure-fire way to get speaking skills. It is also a great way to learn about something. If you have a passion for a subject and you find a way to teach others about it, the chances are you will learn a lot more about it when preparing to speak.

You can volunteer to teach at work, or you can volunteer to teach in other ways. You can teach classes at the library, or you can teach kids in school through programs such as Junior Achievement. You can join a non-profit organization (see above) and then go make presentations to teach others about your group's mission.

Tactic: Join Toastmasters International

Toastmasters is dedicated to helping people learn public speaking and leadership skills. Participants get to practice in a non-threatening environment where they get evaluated on their presentations. The operative word here is *practice.* There are no failures or flops. If you feel like you could have done better in a presentation in Toastmasters, go back the next week and get another chance! You won't get fired or lose a sale.

At Toastmasters, every speech or presentation is evaluated, so you get continuous feedback. You won't get this kind of continuous instruction anywhere else. There are Toastmasters groups in virtually every community. Go to www.toastmasters.org to find a chapter near you.

Tactic: Know how to speak on the spot

If you follow any of the tactics in this section, you may find that you occasionally have to speak on the spot without preparing. Toastmasters groups practice this in an exercise called Table Topics. Speakers are given a subject and they must come up with a one or two minute speech without preparation. The technique to use when you have no time to prepare is an abbreviated version of the Critical

Steps in Part 1. If you must speak with no time to prepare, the following provides a framework to help you:

1. Pause to formulate a response
2. Determine your purpose before you speak
3. Present a few supporting points
4. State your answer, position, or purpose

Learning how to structure your thoughts when you have time for a prepared presentation helps you to know how to answer with little or no notice. For example, a friend of mine was the former president of a local chapter of a trade group. At a meeting a few months after he stepped down from the presidency, he was awarded a gift of thanks and was asked to say a few words. He was not told that he was to receive the gift or be asked to speak. After his genuine initial surprise, he thanked the presenter and addressed the group. He stated three goals he had when he started his term as president and gave the current status of those three goals. He concluded by offering his support to the new president on carrying on those goals and he sat down. It was a great example of a perfectly executed speech crafted on the spot.

Strategy: Avoid the worst mistakes

In my experience of delivering and observing thousands of presentations, here are the ten most common and most detrimental mistakes you can make:

1. *Being unprepared.* Avoiding this mistake is what this book is all about. Too many people try to give a presentation without going through the proper steps to prepare.
2. *Being over-prepared, but under-practiced.* Sometimes people spend too much of their preparation time concentrating on the Critical Steps in Part 1 of this book without spending enough time on Part 2. The result of this is good material and poor delivery.
3. *Having a weak opening.* If a speaker loses the audience in the opening, it is hard to recover. It is not impossible to recover, but it is difficult—and unnecessary.
4. *Reading a script.* Reading a script dramatically changes the tone of the speech or presentation. Unless the words need to be conveyed word for word, they should not be read from a script.
5. *Having a disorganized presentation.* The information has to flow easily for the listeners. If the

speaker jumps around or makes illogical transitions, the audience will have a difficult time staying engaged.

6. *Speaking with an inappropriate volume.* This mistake is almost always not speaking loudly or clearly enough. Speaking in a monotone is also a common mistake. Voice inflection should go up and down as a presentation progresses.
7. *Fearing failure.* The reason many people fear speaking in front of a group is rejection of some kind. However, that rejection rarely comes, especially if the speaker is prepared and practiced.
8. *Not focusing on the audience.* If an audience comes away from a presentation thinking, "So what?" the speaker has not focused enough on the concept of "What's in it for them?"
9. *Too much information.* Sometimes a presentation just has too much information in it. A great presentation should have only the amount of information necessary to convey the points and make the conclusion. Anything more clutters the message and makes the presentation harder to follow. This can make the presentation repetitive and boring.
10. *Having a weak closing.* A weak closing can dissipate the energy created in a presentation. Paraphrasing T. S. Eliot, go out with a bang and not a whimper.

Conclusion

Now that you have read this book, you are fully prepared to plan, prepare, practice, and deliver a speech or presentation for virtually any occasion. Giving a speech or presentation for the first time or in unfamiliar circumstances can be daunting. However, if you follow the critical steps and strategies in this book, I promise you will find that you will give your best speech or presentation ever!

List of Tactics

Tactic: Indicate or signal your intent to close
Tactic: Let your structure help you close
Tactic: Make your closing complement your opening
Tactic: Leave them with something more
Tactic: Avoid these common killer mistakes
Tactic: Be totally prepared
Tactic: Focus on the audience
Tactic: Write down your fears
Tactic: Forget your anxiety
Tactic: Know your opening perfectly
Tactic: Recognize that they can't see your legs shaking
Tactic: Find friends in the audience
Tactic: Remember to breathe
Tactic: Practice out loud
Tactic: Use a mirror
Tactic: Record yourself
Tactic: Practice in front of others
Tactic: Use time wisely
Tactic: Meet and greet the audience
Tactic: Have your host read your introduction
Tactic: Start on time
Tactic: Approach with confidence
Tactic: Use your eyes to open theirs
Tactic: Start with enthusiasm
Tactic: Thank the introducer and address the audience
Tactic: Don't apologize
Tactic: Don't complain
Tactic: Stop on time
Tactic: Reduce or eliminate "crutch" words
Tactic: Over-enunciate for clarity
Tactic: Use short sentences

Tactic: Avoid jargon and acronyms
Tactic: Avoid worn out parts of speech
Tactic: Use voice speed for emphasis
Tactic: Use voice volume to add emphasis
Tactic: Use pauses for dramatic effect
Tactic: Use your hands for emphasis
Tactic: Move around to keep your audience engaged
Tactic: Speak from an outline or bulleted notes
Tactic: Don't read your speech
Tactic: Memorize your entire speech with care
Tactic: Use visual aids as your notes
Tactic: Know when to turn your visual aids on and off
Tactic: Stand to the left of the screen
Tactic: Talk to the audience, not the screen
Tactic: Present the visual, and then pause
Tactic: Be wary of laser pointers
Tactic: Pace your slides
Tactic: Don't apologize for a slide
Tactic: Use traditional visual aids
Tactic: Have a few questions ready
Tactic: Control your Q&A time
Tactic: Thank the questioner
Tactic: Ensure everyone can hear the question
Tactic: Answer for everyone
Tactic: Stay focused in your answers
Tactic: Be aware of the attack question
Tactic: Don't be afraid to say "I don't know"
Tactic: Use Q&A time creatively
Tactic: Have a second closing ready after Q&A
Tactic: Measure your presentation energy level
Tactic: Prepare a condensed version

Tactic: Find a spy or neutralize an enemy
Tactic: Acknowledge audience body language
Tactic: Handle mistakes with care
Tactic: Arrive early to make adjustments
Tactic: Have a backup plan for everything
Tactic: Know where you are on the agenda
Tactic: Have a checklist of items to remember
Tactic: Volunteer
Tactic: Join a civic group
Tactic: Join a non-profit board of directors
Tactic: Volunteer to teach
Tactic: Join Toastmasters International
Tactic: Know how to speak on the spot